UNITED NATIONS OFFICE ON DRUGS AND CRIME

FORUM ON CRIME AND SOCIETY

Volume 3, Numbers 1 and 2, December 2003

Editorial Board:
JAN VAN DIJK
VINCENZO RUGGIERO

Managing Editor:
ANTOINETTE AL-MULLA

International Advisory Board:
KUMARALEVU CHOCKALINGAM (INDIA)
GLORIA EBUGI (NIGERIA)
CYRILLE FIJNAUT (NETHERLANDS)
MARK FINDLAY (AUSTRALIA)
JAMES FINKENAUER (UNITED STATES OF AMERICA)
PETER GASTROW (SOUTH AFRICA)
SVETLANA GLINKINA (RUSSIAN FEDERATION)
FRANCES HEIDENSOHN (UNITED KINGDOM)
ENAMUL HUQ (BANGLADESH)
CELIA LEONES (PHILIPPINES)
MAURICIO RUBIO (COLOMBIA)
SEBASTIAN SCHEERER (GERMANY)
YURI VORONIN (RUSSIAN FEDERATION)
ROBERT WEISS (UNITED STATES OF AMERICA)
XAOWEI ZHANG (CHINA)

UNITED NATIONS
New York, 2004

UNITED NATIONS PUBLICATION
Sales No. E.04.IV.5
ISBN 92-1-130236-6
ISSN 1020-9212

Views expressed in signed articles published in *Forum* are those of the authors and do not necessarily reflect those of the United Nations Secretariat. The designations employed and the presentation of the material in this publication do not imply the expression of any opinion whatsoever on the part of the Secretariat of the United Nations concerning the legal status of any country, territory, city or area or of its authorities, or concerning the delimitation of its frontiers or boundaries.

NOTE FROM THE EDITORIAL BOARD

Forum on Crime and Society is a United Nations sales publication issued by the United Nations Office on Drugs and Crime, based in Vienna. It is published twice yearly in the six official languages of the United Nations: Arabic, Chinese, English, French, Russian and Spanish.

The present issue of *Forum* is devoted to the theme of trends in crime. It is the fourth issue of *Forum* to be published and widely distributed to a varied readership. The first issue (vol. 1, No. 1, February 2001) was devoted to the outcome of the Tenth United Nations Congress on the Prevention of Crime and the Treatment of Offenders, held in Vienna from 10 to 17 April 2000. The second issue (vol. 1, No. 2, December 2001) was devoted to the theme of organized crime, and the third issue (vol. 2, No. 1, December 2002) dealt with corruption.

Forum is available in English on the web site of the United Nations Office on Drugs and Crime (www.unodc.org/unodc/crime_cicp_publications_forum.html).

Readers of *Forum* are invited to complete the interactive Readership Survey Questionnaire posted on the web site.

GUIDELINES FOR THE SUBMISSION OF ARTICLES

The Editorial Board invites scholars and experts from around the world to contribute to *Forum* articles on issues of criminological concern. Articles submitted for publication in *Forum* will be subject to peer review. All manuscripts must be original, that is, they should not have been published elsewhere in part or in whole. The length of manuscripts to be considered for publication as articles in the first section of *Forum* should not exceed 6,000 words. Shorter papers and commentaries to appear in the second section of *Forum*, entitled "Notes and action", should not exceed 2,500 words in length.

Manuscripts should be submitted in hard copy or electronic format and be accompanied by the curriculum vitae of the author and an abstract.

All manuscripts, reviews, enquiries and correspondence should be addressed to Antoinette Al-Mulla, Managing Editor of *Forum*, either by post (United Nations Office on Drugs and Crime, P.O. Box 500, A-1400 Vienna, Austria), by e-mail (Antoinette.Al-Mulla@unvienna.org) or by facsimile (+(43) (1) 26060-5298).

PREFACE

Each of the articles in the present issue of *Forum* deals with the question of how to measure the nature and extent of various forms of criminal activity. There can be little doubt that providing reliable data on global levels of crime, not only specific legally defined types of crime, but also organized crime, corruption, terrorism and illegal trafficking, is the key to effective policy intervention. The articles largely reflect the ongoing work being conducted by the United Nations Office on Drugs and Crime in this respect. It is hoped that policy makers, practitioners and analysts alike will find in this issue of *Forum* not only extensive material for debate, but also a rich supply of data.

In the first article, Edgardo Buscaglia and Jan van Dijk present the results of a study of crime trends focusing on statistical indicators of corruption and various forms of organized crime. They report on the close links between the quality of institutional arrangements, including functioning criminal justice systems, and the levels of organized crime and corruption in a country. Where key state institutions perform poorly, organized crime and corruption thrive and a vicious circle of lawlessness and poverty is created.

Mark Shaw, Jan van Dijk and Wolfgang Rhomberg present an overview of data from the United Nations surveys of crime trends and operations of criminal justice systems, illustrating global reported crime trends since 1980. The article also seeks to provide some data on the effectiveness of criminal justice, as well as a review of global expenditure patterns (presented as a percentage of gross domestic product) on policing. A number of critical recent trends in this respect are highlighted, including the dramatic decline in crime levels in North America in the recent past, as well as the growing problem of levels of interpersonal violent crime in developing countries and in countries with economies in transition.

Roy Walmsley reviews the critical issue of levels of global incarceration. His figures are drawn from data maintained by the United Nations Office on Drugs and Crime and other sources. The article provides a comprehensive and up-to-date review of the state of incarceration across the globe and shows that the development of alternatives to imprisonment remains one of the key challenges facing criminal justice systems today.

In the section of the present issue of *Forum* entitled "Notes and action", five cases are presented in which data collection and analysis are central to ongoing policy debates. The work presented in these contributions reflects, for the most part, work in progress, outlining a series of attempts to collect and analyse data in new ways and new environments and to take concrete steps to implement policies in response to high levels of crime.

In the first article, Kristiina Kangaspunta outlines the preliminary results of an attempt to collect data on trafficking in human beings. She reviews the very real challenges of such data collection and provides an overview of results from the unique database of the United Nations Office on Drugs and Crime on global patterns of such trafficking.

Alex Schmid and Ralph Riachy provide a review of ongoing efforts at juvenile justice reform in Lebanon. They illustrate the impact of the reform (of which data collection is a key component) with an interesting array of statistics, indicating that legislative changes are having some impact within the justice system itself. Their conclusions link to some of the points made in other articles in respect of criminal justice performance and the urgent requirement to develop alternatives to simple incarceration, particularly with respect to young people.

This is followed by an account of the conducting of a locally funded victim survey in a developing country, in this case, in four cities in southern India. K. Chockalingam makes a strong argument (again reinforcing conclusions made in some of the other articles in this issue of *Forum*) that police-recorded crime provides only one perspective (and a limited one at that) on the realities of criminal victimization.

The article by Anna Alvazzi del Frate is a necessary supplement to the presentation of global reported crime figures. It presents results from the International Crime Victim Survey in a large number of countries throughout the world. The Survey provides an independent means of determining crime levels by interviewing citizens about their experience of victimization (when and how it occurred and whether they reported it to the police) as well as their level of satisfaction with police performance.

Finally, Rob Boone, Gary Lewis and Ugljesa Zvekic present a review of crime and potential policy alternatives in Southern Africa. This serves as a useful complement to the articles that point to the serious problem of lawlessness and criminal victimization in sub-Saharan Africa.

It is hoped that this overview may provide some insight into the wide array of topics considered in the present issue of *Forum*. The collection of data at the national, regional and international levels is a key requirement for effective policy interventions aimed at improving citizens' security. It is hoped that the articles presented here constitute a small step in that direction.

The Editorial Board would like to express its appreciation to Rachele Tardi for her help in the preparation of the present issue of *Forum*.

Contents

	Page
Note from the Editorial Board	iii
Guidelines for the submission of articles	iii
Preface	v

Part one.   Articles

Controlling organized crime and corruption in the public sector
  Edgardo Buscaglia and Jan van Dijk 3

Determining global trends in crime and justice: an overview of results from the United Nations surveys of crime trends and operations of criminal justice systems
  Mark Shaw, Jan van Dijk and Wolfgang Rhomberg 35

Global incarceration and prison trends
  Roy Walmsley 65

Part two.   Notes and action

Mapping the inhuman trade: preliminary findings of the database on trafficking in human beings
  Kristiina Kangaspunta 81

Juvenile justice initiatives in Lebanon
  Alex Schmid and Ralph Riachy 105

Criminal victimization in four major cities in southern India
  K. Chockalingam 117

The voice of victims of crime: estimating the true level of conventional crime
  Anna Alvazzi del Frate 127

Measuring and taking action against crime in Southern Africa
  Rob Boone, Gary Lewis and Ugljesa Zvekic 141

PART ONE
Articles

CONTROLLING ORGANIZED CRIME AND CORRUPTION IN THE PUBLIC SECTOR

by Edgardo Buscaglia and Jan van Dijk*

Abstract

Organized crime and corruption are shaped by the lack of strength of the control mechanisms of the State and civil society. The results presented in the present article attest to the links between the growth of organized crime and that of corruption in the public sector in a large number of countries. The two types of complex crime reinforce each other. To identify and isolate the influential factors behind the growth of corruption in the public sector and organized crime, the present article presents and analyses qualitative and quantitative information on a large sample of countries and territories representing worldwide diversity stratified by level of socio-economic development.** The study reported here aimed at identifying the institutional patterns that determine a country's vulnerability to complex crimes. Being policy-oriented, the report includes a set of evidence-based policy recommendations.

INTRODUCTION

Corruption and organized crime are much more than an isolated criminal phenomenon. Theoretical and applied research have shown the interdependent links between the political, socio-economic, criminal justice and

---

*Crime Prevention and Criminal Justice Officer and Officer-in-Charge, Human Security Branch, United Nations Office on Drugs and Crime, respectively. The authors acknowledge the valuable contribution of Kleoniki Balta for her creative inputs in the definition of the variables and development of the database supporting the results presented here and for her capacity to coordinate the efforts of all the participating research assistants. The authors are also grateful to the following research assistants (in chronological order of participation), who were actively involved in collecting, processing and analysing the data: Vendulka Hubachkova, Nicole Maric, Irina Bazarya and Fabrizio Sarrica.

**The study covered a large sample of countries, representing worldwide interregional diversity stratified by level of socio-economic development. It included the following Member States and territories: Albania, Argentina, Australia, Austria, Azerbaijan, Belarus, Belgium, Bolivia, Botswana, Brazil, Bulgaria, Canada, China, Colombia, Costa Rica, Croatia, Czech Republic, Denmark, Estonia, Finland, France, Georgia, Germany, Greece, Hong Kong Special Administrative Region of China, Hungary, India, Indonesia, Ireland, Italy, Jamaica, Japan, Kyrgyzstan, Latvia, Lithuania, Malaysia, Malta, Mongolia, Netherlands, Paraguay, Peru, Philippines, Poland, Portugal, Republic of Korea, Romania, Russian Federation, Singapore, Slovakia, Slovenia, South Africa, Spain, Sweden, Switzerland, Thailand, the former Yugoslav Republic of Macedonia, Uganda, Ukraine, United Kingdom of Great Britain and Northern Ireland, United States of America, Venezuela, Viet Nam, Yugoslavia and Zimbabwe.

legal domains [1-2]. The present article explores those determining factors, relying upon several operational variables that reflect the prevailing institutional features of each country. Institutional linkages to organized crime and corruption in the public sector are first identified through a simple correlation analysis that does not necessarily imply causal effects. Factor analysis coupled with the application of multiple regression techniques narrows down the most important set of institutional linkages. The analysis was founded entirely on the development of corruption and organized crime indicators.

Towards a composite index of corruption in the public sector

The aim of the work presented here was to develop an index of corruption to be used in statistical analyses for policy purposes. "Corruption" is defined broadly as "the abuse of public power for private gain". To assess the prevalence of street-level corruption, the study used an indicator compiled by the International Crime Victim Survey that records the frequency with which citizens experience actual requests for bribes. Data from the Survey cover mainly the types of street- and medium-level corruption that an average citizen faces in his or her dealings with public agencies (appendix E, table 77).* The indicator does not include high-level corruption, which is a form of grand corruption, but refers to the extent and frequency with which private interests penetrate the institutions of the State and bias public policies in their favour. A composite index was constructed in order to measure high-level corruption. Perceptional indicators were compiled on distortions arising from interest groups, the independence of policies from the pressures of special interest groups, the likelihood of biased judicial rulings, perceptions of the percentage of the value of public procurement-related contracts paid for bribes and of the prevalence of "state capture" (appendix E, table 78).

Towards a composite index of organized crime

To measure the prevalence of organized crime, the study used an index that combined objective factors linked with complex crimes. The development of an international index of organized crime obviously had to start

---

*Statistical tables showing the results of the study presented here can be found at www.unodc.org/unodc/crime/crime_cicp_publications_forum.html and are referred to in parentheses in the present article.

from a universally agreed upon definition. During the 1990s, law enforcement agencies in Europe developed a number of operational definitions of the term "organized criminal group". Those definitions agree on the following crucial elements: such a group is structured, has some permanence, commits serious crimes for profit, uses violence, corrupts officials, launders criminal proceeds and reinvests in the licit economy.

The United Nations Convention against Transnational Organized Crime (General Assembly resolution 55/25, annex I) defines an organized criminal group as "a structured group, committing serious crimes for profit".* That very broad definition was favoured over the listing of the most common types of organized crime such as trafficking in drugs, arms, persons, stolen cars or protected species and terrorism. The Convention thus focuses on the same types of group as are targeted by law enforcement agencies using the Falcone checklist, which was later incorporated into the so-called Falcone framework.** This is evident from the three protocols supplementary to the Convention, dealing with trafficking in persons, smuggling of migrants and trafficking in firearms (General Assembly resolutions 55/25, annexes I and II, and 55/250, annex), as well as from provisions in the Convention dealing with such secondary characteristics of organized crime as the use of corruption, violence, money-laundering and reinvestment in the licit economy.

For the purposes of calculating the organized crime index used here, the extent of organized crime in a country was assessed on the basis of indicators of the various defining elements contained both in operational investigations conducted by law enforcement agencies (e.g. the Falcone checklist) and in the Organized Crime Convention and its protocols. It was also concluded that official data on police records of criminal activities offered little reliable information on the extent of organized crime activity in a country and that other sources would have to be found or developed.

One potentially relevant source is the World Economic Forum's survey of business aimed at measuring the costs imposed by organized crime on firms [3], which provides an estimate of the extent of victimization of businesses by organized crime. The country ranking based on the World Economic Forum's index was subsequently correlated with indices for

---

*The United Nations Convention against Transnational Organized Crime and the protocols thereto are available at www.unodc.org/unodc/crime_cicp_convention.html

**The Falcone checklist provides an operational account of organized criminal groups operating within a certain jurisdiction by describing the composition, structure, modus operandi, licit/illicit linkages and other important aspects necessary for the investigation and prosecution of criminal networks. For more details, see S. Gonzalez-Ruiz and E. Buscaglia (2002) [2].

corruption and violence (homicide). The three indices were found to be highly correlated across a group of 70 countries and, as a result, a composite index of non-conventional crime was constructed [4-5].

It was subsequently decided to seek additional available country data on the core activities of organized criminal groups such as credit card fraud and trafficking in drugs, persons, firearms, stolen cars and cigarettes.* The indicator for drug trafficking (police seizure data) did not show any correlation with the other organized crime factors mentioned above and was subsequently excluded from the analysis. Finally, a composite index was constructed that included indicators of five core activities (trafficking in persons, firearms, stolen cars and cigarettes and fraud) and four secondary factors (costs for business, extent of the informal economy as a proportion of gross domestic product, violence and money-laundering). This composite index of organized crime is used in the analysis below. It should be noted that although the composite index has proved to be robust and not much affected by the inclusion or exclusion of individual indicators, efforts are nevertheless ongoing to add further statistical indicators. The purpose of the study was to derive policy recommendations addressing institutional reform through a process of identifying best practices across the globe. For that reason the study profiles the countries involved according to several features, which—for practical reasons—are classified into six broad areas: *(a)* socio-economic factors; *(b)* the political sphere; *(c)* the criminal justice system; *(d)* private sector governance; *(e)* public sector governance; and *(f)* independence and integrity of the judiciary (appendix I.A).

The objective of the study was not to offer a new theory of organized crime, but to focus on the exploration and empirical verification (or re-examination) of the links existing between organized crime and its main

---

*In particular, data were compiled on smuggling of firearms (taking into account data on manufacturing, sales, imports and exports already computed by the United Nations), estimates on smuggling of cigarettes, car theft and consumer fraud victimization (the International Crime Victim Survey), number of homicides (the United Nations, the International Criminal Police Organization (Interpol) and the World Health Organization), size of the informal economy and the business sector's perceptions of organized crime prevalence (World Economic Forum), inflows of laundered money in millions of dollars per year as a proportion of gross domestic product (the Walker index) and trafficking in persons in terms of nationalities of suspects (human trafficking database of the United Nations Office on Drugs and Crime). The index presented here ranked each country for each variable in order to compute the composite organized crime index as an average of the rankings that each country showed for each item mentioned above. Each component showed strong correlations with the index, with costs to business, homicide and money-laundering being the best predictors. The index considered here only included those countries for which there were at least three observations out of which at least two were "core activity" factors. Higher values corresponded to greater prevalence of organized crime (appendix E, table 79).

economic, administrative, legal-judicial and political causes. Those links were first identified through simple correlation analysis and the main results are presented below.

Socio-economic factors

In many cases poverty and unemployment do not just provide a greater supply of potential illegal labour for organized criminal activities, but they also create a favourable environment for criminals to exploit the social fabric of countries as a foundation for organized crime. In some cases (in the south of Italy, for example), organized crime forces legal businesses to generate employment for a fee paid to criminal syndicates in the area. Thus organized crime is actually playing a positive social role, as a dispenser of services. Moreover, organized crime also grows as a result of the failure of the State to provide dispute resolution mechanisms on labour matters or when the State fails to assure access to legal services or to financial markets.

Based on a statistical analysis of the sample of countries covered in the present study, organized crime has the capacity to take advantage of poor economic and social conditions within a country (appendix A, table 1). For example, all indicators measuring the effectiveness of the State in fighting monopolistic practices have a negative correlation with organized crime. The same applies to indicators measuring the degree of economic freedom enjoyed (appendix A, tables 1-3).

The degree of openness of an economy, expressed by the scale and scope of regulations applied to foreign trade, and openness to imports and foreign direct investment were all considered. All those features are inversely related to the organized crime index. This suggests that openness to foreign trade or investment is important in permitting new economic forces to challenge incumbents within domestic markets and to undermine the old economic capture of a territory by organized crime (appendix A, table 3).

A lack of clear definition and enforcement of property rights is associated with higher levels of organized crime. This confirms the findings of Milhaupt and West [6] applied to Italy, Japan and the Russian Federation. In the present much larger sample of countries, when there is no clear definition of property rights, organized crime then plays its key "authority" role, setting its own rules in areas such as credit allocation, labour disputes or in "protecting" property for a fee (appendix A, table 3).

The tax system is an important economic dimension that has a major impact on organized criminal activities. An environment where tax evasion is prevalent is often accompanied by the higher levels of organized crime associated with the nature and scale of money-laundering (appendix A, table 1).

The financial and monetary structure of a country also affects a country's risk rating: analysis shows that a country's financial and liquidity risk ratings are all positively related to the organized crime index. One can conclude that higher country risk ratings are associated with higher levels of organized crime (appendix A, table 2). Conversely, a low risk rating indicates effective and functioning financial monitoring of economic interactions, good protection of large and small investors and effective functioning of central banks or of other legal authorities that manage to instil overall transparency into markets.

The quality of a State's economic management can be assessed by its three main economic policies, fiscal, monetary and trade policies. A governance quality index has been constructed on that basis by Huther and Shah [7]. The strong correlation with the organized crime index used here suggests that high quality of economic management is important in providing an environment that is less conducive to organized criminal activities (appendix A, table 2).

The political sphere

Organized crime and democracy work according to guiding principles that are in direct conflict with one another. A democratic State upholds the sovereignty of the nation and ensures the protection of the rights of all individuals, regardless of wealth, social status, age or gender. Organized crime as traditionally defined, on the other hand, is built around patronage, carrying on a tradition of feudalism, and does not hesitate to commit human rights abuses.

An analysis of the relationship between organized crime and the democratic State finds that the growth of one negatively affects the growth of the other, that is, consolidation of democracy taking place concomitantly at the local and national levels impedes the growth of organized crime (appendix A, tables 4 and 5).

However, even in a democratic political framework where institutionalized mechanisms for governing and distributing public goods, including justice, do exist, there is still a danger of penetration of those state institutions by organized crime, a phenomenon that is described as "state capture". The way in which organized crime usually "captures" the State is by coopting public institutions. In contrast to the standard forms of corruption, high-level corruption represents a more sophisticated, more pernicious form, which frequently leads to enactment of "suitable" state decisions creating a bias in the design and implementation of public policies. The relationship between state capture and organized crime was examined in the present study and the results showed that the two phenomena were strongly linked, meaning that higher levels of state capture are associated with the spread of organized crime (appendix A, table 4).

Criminal justice system

The criminal justice system of a country is a key factor in any analysis of how effective the State is in responding to serious crimes, in particular organized crime. What surfaced from initial analyses here was that the number of personnel employed in police and prosecution services was positively correlated with levels of organized crime (appendix A, table 6). The immediate explanation is that, in countries with high crime rates, the first response of the State is to increase the number of police personnel, therefore the higher the crime rate, the more personnel the country will need to come to terms with the problem. More generally, that trend is also confirmed, if the financial resources invested in a criminal justice system are considered (appendix A, table 6). In that analytical context, the size of the payroll and the money spent on criminal justice is positively related to the level of organized crime.

The study presented here also considered measurements of the effectiveness of criminal justice systems. It is noteworthy that an international index of total recorded crimes per capita is related inversely to the level of organized crime (appendix A, table 7). In countries with lower levels of organized crime, higher percentages of drug arrests are recorded (appendix A, table 8). In countries with high levels of organized crime, the criminal justice system may not be able to deal adequately with crimes committed and official statistics may thus not reflect the actual nature and scale of crimes perpetrated. On the other hand, when a criminal justice system works properly, in terms, for example, of more arrests and convictions for drug trafficking, that institutional effectiveness helps to control organized crime better. In many countries with less than effective law enforcement institutions, victims lack confidence in state institutions and so citizens rarely report crimes or request police intervention. In such environments, citizens often find support in illegal organizations, such as mafia-type groups, to deal with minor crimes. Ironically, then, low levels of recorded crimes and drug arrests in a country may point to low effectiveness of the police and a relatively high prevalence of organized crime.

In order to come to terms with the above constraints, the present study proposed a more direct measure of effectiveness of criminal justice, consisting of computing the ratio of victimization by common crime derived from the International Crime Victim Survey [8] divided by the number of convictions per capita. A smaller ratio can be seen as a measure of effectiveness of criminal justice since it reflects higher risks of punishment for offenders per crime committed. After correlating the measure of such effectiveness with the organized crime index, a clear association emerged between the two variables (appendix A, table 9), that is, the level of organized crime is lower in countries where the conviction rates per crimes committed are higher. In other words, the presumed deterrent effect of functioning criminal justice systems with regard to organized crime is clearly demonstrated in the present analysis.

The largest return for expenditure invested in criminal justice systems may lie in the training of specialized personnel. When countries introduce training and organizational control of decision-making processes through special anti-organized crime units (i.e. higher levels of training allocated to their anti-organized crime officers and prosecutors), significant reductions in organized crime can be observed [2].

Private sector governance

Lack of private sector governance provides a breeding ground for the growth of organized crime. The study reported here approaches private sector governance from two perspectives. The first perspective refers to the question of how transparent and effective the banking system is and how feasible it is for business to access financial services within a formal regulatory framework in order to conduct its normal activities. If small or large businesses find it difficult to obtain loans, they will rely on illegal sources for the provision of financial services at higher interest rates (usury). The statistical results confirm this (appendix A, table 12).

The second perspective concerns the governance of the financial sector and corporations, focusing in particular on the anti-money-laundering legislation coupled with a regulatory framework and banking supervision practices. In accordance with the Euroshore study [9], it is possible to rank countries in terms of the enactment and implementation of their anti-money-laundering legislation coupled with their regulatory practices and banking supervision. The present study indicates that in countries with low regulatory standards applied to banks, the organized crime index doubles compared with countries with higher standards of enforcement of anti-money-laundering legislation (appendix A, table 11). This analysis is supplemented by the indicators of perception of transparency of financial institutions, coupled with the level of financial disclosure required (appendix A, table 12). All these indices correlate inversely with organized crime.

Regarding the enforcement of accounting standards, analysis takes into account the nature and scope of the information requested by law from private companies in accordance with an index compiled by the Center for International Law and Economic Development at the University of Virginia School of Law. Seven categories are considered (general financial information, income statements, balance sheets, fund flow statements, accounting standards, stock data and special items). In the present study it was found that the organized crime index was also inversely related to good accounting standards applied to private businesses (appendix A, table 12).

Public sector governance

"Buying" protection from the State is a necessary condition for the growth of organized crime. To measure the degree of corruptibility of the public domain, the level of state capture was measured, which, as was reported for the political sphere, is related to the organized crime index. Additionally, the independence of civil servants from political pressure was examined and it was found that higher levels of political intervention in the appointment, dismissal and promotion of civil servants went hand in hand with higher levels of organized criminal activity (appendix A, table 13).

Another pernicious effect can be traced to the distortions caused by interest groups (appendix A, table 14). Lobbying can be conducted through legal means, as a way to influence the making of laws, regulations and policies. Nevertheless, organized crime can also "lobby" the State in its quest to block or to enact laws for its own purposes. Customs offices provide an excellent example of such interference: customs bureaux are responsible for allowing for access of goods and services into a country and play a key role in preventing both trafficking in persons and drugs and smuggling of goods and services in general. As a result, customs are well worth being "captured" by organized crime. The finding of the present study in that regard was that lower effectiveness of customs systems was related to higher levels of organized crime (appendix A, table 13).

Independence and integrity of the judiciary

Analysis shows that judicial independence is strongly related to levels of organized crime. Results also show a strong correlation between the perceived independence of the judiciary and the perceived extent of judicial corruption (appendix A, table 16). Statistical analysis confirmed here that independent judges were less vulnerable to corruption and better able to implement repressive actions against organized crime, even when the political system and other areas of the State had been captured by organized crime. In that context, for example, corrupt judges were found to abuse their substantive and procedural discretion through rulings that slowed down or obstructed law enforcement in organized criminal cases (appendix A, table 15).

Among the factors making it possible for organized crime to capture the court system, the most significant are procedural complexity and abuses of substantive judicial discretion. The present analysis verified those links (e.g. that higher degrees of procedural complexity were linked to judicial corruption and to higher levels of organized crime) (appendix A, tables 15-17). The link between the abuse of substantive judicial discretion on the one hand and judicial corruption and increases in organized crime on the other was confirmed through another analysis. Moreover, lack of predictability of judicial rulings was linked[x] to higher levels of both court corruption and organized criminal activities (appendix A, table 16).

A multi-variable analysis of key correlates of organized crime

In order to identify which of the many correlates of organized crime found are the best predictors of the level of organized crime, multiple regression analysis was applied, with the organized crime index acting as the dependent variable. The recommendations made below are based on the strongest variables as determined by the correlation analyses (appendix A, table 18). The selection of independent variables was guided by the need to include as many of the areas considered above as possible (i.e. socio-economic factors, the political sphere, the criminal justice system, private sector governance, public sector governance and independence and integrity of the judiciary). The choice of variables was also supported by the results of the factor analyses (appendix F, table 87). Variables that best represented their particular domains were chosen for inclusion in the regression models.

Several regression models were able to explain 50 per cent or more of the variance in the organized crime index scores. A multiple regression model including the human development index (representing socio-economic factors; also included as control variable), independence of the judiciary (representing the judicial integrity area) and police protection of property rights (representing the effectiveness of the criminal justice system) explained 72 per cent of the variations in the organized crime index, as shown in table 1 below (see also appendix F, table 84).

Table 1. Multiple regression analysis of organized crime

Variables	Independence of the judiciary	Police protection	Human development index
Beta (standard coefficient)	−.378	−.437	−.236
Significance	.008	.001	.065

Model summary[a]

Model	R	R square
1	.718[b]	.515
2	.825[c]	.681
3	.849[d]	.720

[a]Dependent variable: organized crime index.
[b]Predictors (constant): independence of the judiciary from political pressure.
[c]Predictors (constant): independence of the judiciary from political pressure and police protection of property rights from criminal action.
[d]Predictors (constant): independence of the judiciary from political pressure, police protection of property rights from criminal action and human development index 1999.

The results indicated that independence and integrity of the judiciary was the most important predictor of the extent of organized crime. Independently of this, the extent of organized crime was higher in countries where the police were less effective. Finally, organized crime was more prevalent in less affluent countries, independently of the two other factors. On the basis of these three key factors, levels of organized crime per country could be predicted fairly accurately. The result leaves little doubt about the importance of law enforcement and criminal justice in the fight against organized crime.

Results on corruption in the public sector

Socio-economic factors

Socio-economic factors include the wealth of a country, the distribution of national income and how the public revenues are invested in the overall structure of the State, which fundamentally shapes the quality of life of the population. High levels of national income mean added financial resources to support the criminal justice system. It comes as no surprise that high levels of national income and development were associated with lower levels of both street-level corruption (appendix C, table 22) and high-level corruption (appendix C, table 23).*

Evidence suggests that tax and customs administrations are usually among the most corruption-prone government agencies, especially in developing countries. When tax evasion is rampant among businesses and individuals as a result of lax controls, public servants verifying the illegalities can be "bought". In that case both subjects will gain: the entrepreneur will continue to pay lower taxes, while the controller will receive extra money. An inadequate tax system, or a system perceived as such, is not only an incentive for tax evasion, which reduces public revenues but, as confirmed by the present analysis, also increases corruption (appendix C, tables 23 and 24).

It is also necessary to explore the links between the degree of economic freedom of a country and the spread of corruption. Economic freedom means fewer contacts between private economic operators and state institutions; hence fewer opportunities for corruption arise. More economic freedom also means greater competition and fewer barriers applied to the economic interaction among physical and legal persons, thus making it harder to build privileged relations based on vested interests (appendix C, tables 23 and 25). All these aspects are inversely correlated with corruption. The amount of protectionism and levels of foreign direct investment were also examined and the results showed that a more open domestic market was linked to less street-level and high-level corruption (appendix C, tables 26 and 27).

---

*Development and corruption can affect each other in a feedback loop mode. The Asian Development Bank has conducted studies that have shown how corruption can cost a country up to 17 per cent of its gross domestic product, robbing the population of resources that can be used to reduce poverty and promote sustainable development.

Independence and integrity of the judiciary

The legal environment, and in particular the way the judiciary functions and the quality of the services provided, has been acknowledged as one of the most significant determinants of corruption [11]. This is due to the fact that only an independent, fairly administered and predictable judiciary can fulfil its role as institutional guarantor of the rule of law, assuring that wrongdoers are punished with a high degree of predictability. Moreover, since much of the corruption in the public sector involves medium-level and high-ranking office holders and politicians, a necessary condition for repressing such criminal behaviour seems to lie with the judiciary, as they are assigned the important task of making sure that members of the Government do not act outside the law. In the present analysis, independence and fairness of the judiciary emerged as the single most important determinant of both street-level and high-level corruption in the public sector (appendix C, tables 28 and 29).

Procedural complexity serves as a barrier to access to court services and to justice in general. In order to develop an approximate measure of procedural complexity, which normally leads to court delays, a legal formalism index already used in previous applied research conducted by Lopez de Silanes [12] was used here. The results of the present study showed a strong link between higher levels of corruption and both proxies for higher procedural complexity, thus confirming the original hypothesis (appendix C, table 30).

The criminal justice system

The resources allocated to criminal justice systems must be expected to have an impact on levels of corruption. The underlying assumption is that the more personnel and money are employed in curbing crime, the more effective will be the performance of the relevant agencies in fighting corruption. One way or another the effectiveness and efficient functioning of the criminal justice system should affect corruption levels, since, as already stated, corruption is a crime involving the rational assessment of potential costs and benefits by those who commit such acts.

Initial correlation analysis showed a strong association between frequency of corruption incidence and rate (per 100,000 people) of personnel allocated to police and prosecution (appendix C, table 33). The correlation was positive, indicating that the higher the numbers of human resources in those agencies, the higher the incidence of low-level and high-level corruption (appendix C, table 34). Similar results were found with regard to organized crime. Analysis also showed a positive link between money spent on law enforcement and a measure of serious complex crimes as measured by the corruption indicators (appendices A, table 6, and C, table 37).

The study then examined the number of crimes per 100,000 inhabitants, the number of prosecutions per 100,000 inhabitants, the number of criminal cases brought before criminal courts per 100,000 inhabitants and the number of convictions for any type of crime per 100,000 inhabitants (appendix C, tables 38 and 39). The results showed that higher output-related effectiveness of the criminal justice system was correlated with lower levels of corruption. The ratio between number of convictions per capita and the rate of victimization by common crimes among the public according to the International Crime Victim Survey was calculated. This measure of criminal justice effectiveness, which was also used in the analysis of organized crime, was strongly inversely related with high-level corruption (appendix C, table 40). The hypothesis that deterrence is higher the more convictions are effected per crime committed seems also to be supported by cross-national analysis with regard to corruption.

The political sphere

Non-democratic regimes are in part sustained by loyal "courts" exercising in most cases undue authority in order to keep and widen their illegitimate political power. Such a mechanism works through the biased selection and promotion of personnel [13]. To confirm those hypotheses, countries were classified in terms of the presence of public officials, recruitment practices and competitiveness. Bureaucracies that show less meritocracy experience higher levels of corrupt practice (appendix C, table 61).

The study also examined the connection between corruption and a country's democratic tradition involving higher levels of social capital. Daniel Treisman [14] has hypothesized that corruption will be lower in democratic countries and those with a freer press and more vigorous civic associations. Countries with a stronger democratic tradition and with larger stocks of social capital, experience, at the same time, lower rates of high- and low-level corruption (appendix C, tables 41 and 43). There is also a direct relationship between interruptions in the democratic processes (e.g political instability) and corrupt practices. The results here confirmed, for example, that more intense armed conflicts were associated with higher levels of corruption (appendix C, table 44).

Given that democratic countries with high stocks of social capital tend to experience lower levels of corruption, how is it that consolidated democracies still often experience political corruption? Responding to this question requires investigation of the nature and scope of the constraints applied to the decision-making power of public officials. Operationally, this variable refers to the decision-making powers of chief executives. Limits to the discretion of public officials also represent an increase in their accountability. In general, data analysis showed that a balanced use of constraints tended to reduce the likelihood of corrupt practices (appendix C, table 45).

The most "institutional" instrument for accountability in democracies is the electoral system. Electoral mechanisms have been classified into four major groups: plurality, majority, semi-proportional and proportional [15]. The present study found that there was more corruption in countries having a proportional type of electoral system than any other type (appendix C, table 46). In particular, there was higher corruption within proportional systems, especially in closed-list representation systems where there were poor links between voters and politicians and thus less incentive for politicians to translate social preferences into political action.

The nature, scale and scope of public information channels are highly relevant for the maintenance of democracy, since a well-informed electorate can hold its politicians accountable for illegal activities, including corruption. More specifically, statistical analysis shows that higher levels of media activity are correlated to lower levels of corruption: information seems to be an important controlling force in anti-corruption programmes (appendices C, table 47, and D, table 73). Media and information flows can also be biased and/or "bought" by political and economic concentrations of power. Less competition in the media sector thus enhances the spread of corruption. To verify this hypothesis, the statistical analysis undertaken examined the percentage of state-owned daily newspapers as a measure of state ownership of the press. It was found that higher proportions of the media owned by the State were related to higher levels of street-level and high-level corruption (appendix C, tables 48 and 49).

Private sector governance

Corruption in the private sector is encouraged by the maintenance of low standards of accounting practices, such as keeping off-the-books accounts and non-accountable funds. Such lax accounting not only means lower taxes, since profits are kept hidden, but can also hide the presence of slush funds for illegal practices, feeding into systemic corruption. In such cases, businesses are usually in connivance with public officials. The study presented here examined the connection between corruption and a country's maintenance of accounting standards in a sample of 60 countries, using the University of Virginia index (see above), which covers the degree of reporting on several items, such as general financial information, income statements, balance sheets, fund flow statements, accounting standards, stock data and special items. The results showed that stronger enforcement of detailed accounting standards was associated with lower levels of corruption (appendix C, table 50).

Where financial regulations are not strictly enforced, there are likely to be many cases of bribery. The present study examined the relationship between corruption and the enforcement of banking and security regulations (appendices A, table 12, and C, table 50) and the results suggested that stronger enforcement of banking and security regulations was associated with lower levels of corruption.

Public sector governance

Several studies have already made reference to the empirical links between administrative inefficiency-ineffectiveness and corruption [16]. In this section some of the main factors of good public governance linked to the control of public sector corruption are discussed. The analysis performed first linked administrative corruption with perceptions of the quality of bureaucracy. The results were convincing (appendix C, table 57).

In order to study the relationships between patronage, the quality of bureaucracy and corruption, proxies measuring the presence of a politicized bureaucracy were linked with two perceptional indicators, "independence of the civil service from political pressure" and "immunity of the public service from political interference". The hypothesis that enhanced independence of civil servants is related to higher quality of the bureaucracy and to lower levels of corruption was also verified (appendix C, tables 58 and 59). Additionally, high-level corruption was found to be strongly correlated with the variables "independence of civil service from political pressure" and "immunity of public service from political interference" (appendix C, table 60).

Furthermore, the impact of economic interventionism of States on rates of high-level corruption is significant. State intervention in the private sector, that is, the extent to which the State interferes in economic interactions within the private domain, comes in many forms, one of which is the granting of government subsidies to private companies. High levels of corruption are associated with high distortions and abuse of discretion in the granting of state subsidies to the private sector (appendix C, table 60).

Procurement has been recognized as a high-risk area, since it frequently involves huge sums of public monies flowing to the private sector based on decisions by public officials. In some cases, corrupt transactions are the norm as a result of common institutional failures that could be avoided, an assumption that was tested by running correlations between perceptional indicators on procurement opened to foreign bidders and the index of high-level corruption, which proved to be significantly strong (appendix C, table 60). More discretion exercised by public officials is also associated with higher levels of corruption in procurement.

Another government sector usually characterized as corruption-prone is customs. The association was examined between the spread of corruption in this area and two perceptional variables measuring whether the "customs bureaucracy hinders the efficient transit of goods" and "efficiency of customs". Statistics showed a negative correlation between corruption and the quality of the customs bureaucracy and their efficiency, measured in terms of procedural complexity and abuse of discretion exercised by customs officials in the exercise of their duties (appendix C, tables 60 and 63). In short, high-quality customs are associated with lower levels of corruption.

Regulation is one of many key areas where the interests of business people and regulators stand in sharp contrast and many opportunities and justifications for corruption arise. Since the great number of required procedures not only increases the chances for public officials to initiate or respond to corrupt transactions (opportunity factor/supply side) but also "forces" businessmen to adopt such corrupt practices in order to "jump the queues" (demand side), the study examined the association between corruption prevalence and red tape, represented by the number of procedures required in order to start a new business. The statistical link between increased red tape and higher corruption proves to be positive and very strong (appendix C, table 64).

Corruption can be seen as a way to accelerate administrative procedures for those willing to pay bribes or "speed money". Extraction of undue benefits, such as rents, by politicians and/or regulators in many cases takes the form of outright extortion. This can happen, for example, when regulators impose delays or repeated obstacles on private firms until a bribe is paid [17]. The association between the prevalence of corruption and the time spent with bureaucrats, as represented by the number of business days required in order to obtain authorization to start a firm, was examined. The links between the two variables proved to be very significant (appendix C, table 64). The relationship showed that the more time required, the greater the corruption involved. Analysis suggested a strong positive association between high-level corruption and regulation of entry in terms of numbers of procedures, time and cost involved (appendix C, table 67). That is, excessive red tape was associated with a higher level of corruption.

An essential characteristic of good governance is the existence and efficient functioning of institutions that hold public officials accountable. State bureaucracies can be made accountable to the political executive (ministerial responsibility), to the legislative assembly (legislative oversight), to the public (ombudsman, media) or to the judiciary. Judicial scrutiny of the bureaucracy is found in systems where administrative law is established as a separate branch of public law. In many States, this leads to the creation of a network of administrative courts empowered to resolve disputes between the government bureaucracy and private citizens. The existence of such bodies is not of itself a guarantee of low administrative crime, but when they are proved to be effective, then corruption is less frequent. Lower rates of corruption appear in systems with higher rates of litigation against government (the likelihood of winning a dispute filed against the Government or a state agency) and greater compensation for state intervention (the existence of the legal right to seek compensation from the State for damages incurred as a result of unlawful state interference) (appendix C, tables 68 and 69).

Multi-variable analysis of the key correlates of corruption

In order to determine the best predictors of low-level and high-level corruption, multiple regression models were used for the most important variables shown by correlation analysis (appendix C, tables 70 and 71) while also taking into account the results of the factor analyses (appendix F, table 87). This was done by considering as independent variables representative proxies of private sector governance, public governance, independence and integrity of the judiciary, the criminal justice system and socio-economic factors, respectively.

The results of the multiple regression model showed that low levels of corruption were affected by levels of judicial independence (judicial integrity), the levels of the United Nations human development index (as regards socio-economic factors), the independence of civil servants (public governance) and the strength of democratic institutions (in the political sphere), as shown in table 2. The four factors together explained 88 per cent of the variations in street-level corruption in the cross-country sample and together allowed for almost perfect prediction of the level of common corruption in a country.

Table 2. Multiple regression analysis of low-level corruption

Variables	Independence of the judiciary	Human development index	Independence of civil servants	Polity
Beta (standard coefficient)	–.893	–.688	–.481	.247
Significance	.008	.001	.034	.035

Model summary[a]

Model	R	R square
1	.832[b]	.693
2	.861[c]	.741
3	.890[d]	792
4	.909[e]	.826

[a]Dependent variable: low-level corruption (data derived from the International Crime Victim Survey (cities only) of 1999 or, if not available, from that of 1995.

[b]Predictor (constant): independence of the judiciary from political pressure.

[c]Predictors (constant): independence of the judiciary from political pressure and human development index 1999.

[d]Predictors (constant): independence of the judiciary from political pressure, human development index 1999 and independence of civil servants from political pressure.

[e]Predictors (constant): independence of the judiciary from political pressure, human development index 1999, independence of civil servants from political pressure and polity.

The same multiple regression method was used in considering high-level corruption as the dependent variable. The following independent variables showed the most significant relationships: "foreign trade regulation" (in the socio-economic area), "enforcement of banking regulation" (private governance), "quality of the bureaucracy" (public governance) and "polity levels" (in the political sphere), as shown in table 3. The four factors accounted for 89 per cent of the variation in high-level corruption across countries.

Table 3. Multiple regression analysis of high-level corruption

Variables	Enforcement of banking regulations	Polity	Quality of the bureaucracy	Openness to foreign trade
Beta (standard coefficient)	−.246	−.231	−.346	−.268
Significance	.097	.069	.014	.026

Model summary[a]

Model	R	R square
1	.833[b]	.695
2	.894[c]	.799
3	.921[d]	.848
4	.942[e]	.887

[a]Dependent variable: high-level corruption (state capture index).
[b]Predictor (constant): enforcement of banking regulations.
[c]Predictors (constant): enforcement of banking regulations and polity.
[d]Predictors (constant): enforcement of banking regulations, polity and quality of the bureaucracy.
[e]Predictors (constant): enforcement of banking regulations, polity, quality of the bureaucracy and openness to foreign trade.

The results of the above regression analyses were robust and significant for each of the selected independent variables (appendix F, tables 85 and 86). By using the sets of variables mentioned, the levels of corruption per country could be predicted with reasonably small margins of error.

Policy recommendations

Discussion now turns to how organized crime and corruption can be reduced by strengthening state institutions and involving civil society.

The organized crime-corruption nexus

Analysis confirmed a very strong level of association between the index for levels of organized crime and the index for public sector corruption, as demonstrated in table 4. Rampant corruption offers opportunities for organized crime that are readily exploited by emerging criminal groups. When organized crime acquires a dominant position, corruption within the public sector is bound to grow. The many ways in which organized crime and corruption in the public sector "feed" each other justify examining both types of complex crime in a joint manner in parallel with the policy recommendations below, which include examples of successful national experiences in the fight against organized crime and corruption in the public sector.

Table 4. Correlations

	Spearman's rho	Organized crime index	Low-level corrruption[a]	High-level corruption (state capture index)
Organized crime index	Correlation coefficient Significance (two-tailed) N[c]	1.000 — 58	0.688[b] 0.000 44	0.708[b] 0.000 50
Low-level corruption "ICVS, city" 1999 (if not, 1995)	Correlation coefficient Significance (two-tailed) N[c]	0.688[b] 0.000 44	1.000[b] — 48	0.698[b] 0.000 37
High-level corruption (state capture index)	Correlation coefficient Significance (two-tailed) N[c]	0.708[b] 0.000 50	0.698[b] 0.000 37	1.000 — 67

[a] Data derived from the International Crime Victim Survey (cities only) of 1999 or, if not available, from that of 1995.
[b] Correlation is significant at the .01 level (two-tailed).
[c] Number of countries sampled.

In this context, five levels of infiltration of the public sector by organized crime need to be addressed by policy makers. The first level involves sporadic acts of bribery or abuse of public office at low levels of government agencies by organized crime. The second level involves acts of corruption occurring on a frequent basis by having low-ranking state officials on the organized criminal payroll. The third level occurs when organized crime infiltrates the managerial domain of public agencies in an attempt, for example, to bias the hiring of state personnel in order to favour the operations of criminal groups. The fourth level of infiltration compromises the heads of agencies responsible directly or indirectly for fighting organized crime-related activities (e.g. drug enforcement agencies) or may involve cases of agencies providing potential long-term benefits to a criminal group (e.g. customs). This fourth level represents an increased perniciousness with long-term negative effects on the capacity of the State to eradicate corruption and organized crime. Finally, the fifth level of infiltration by organized crime encompasses the capture of the State's policies by criminal groups who are then able to bias law making, law enforcement and judicial decisions themselves. This fifth type of state infiltration involves high-level officials such as senators, ministers or even presidents of countries usually compromised by organized criminal groups in order to bias policy-making. At this fifth level of infiltration, organized crime is involved in the campaign financing of politicians or through other more common types of extortion and family links to high-level officials. Such state capture represents the highest level of corruption in the public sector, which paves the way for the expansion and consolidation of transnational organized crime.

Criminal justice reforms: legislative issues and investigative tools

In order to implement successfully the "right" types of legal and criminal justice policy reform against the combination of organized crime and corruption in the public sector, States must first ensure that appropriate legal instruments are in place.

In the legal domain, a few countries have pioneered the enactment of legal measures that criminalize conspiracy to commit a crime. Other countries criminalize membership or participation in criminal enterprises. Illicit association as a form of criminal activity has been introduced into many criminal codes around the world, in particular those of France, Italy, Spain and States in Latin America. Other countries have established as criminal offences crimes committed by groups. In Italy these are called "associated crimes" or "Mafia-type crimes". In the United States of America, legislators have enacted the Racketeer Influenced and Corrupt Organizations Statute (the so-called RICO statute), which prohibits engaging in an enterprise involved in a pattern of criminal activity (racketeering). In that case, judicial rulings indicate that a "RICO enterprise" entails an organizational structure that carries on its business by means of activities that are primarily criminal and where there is a high degree of probability that the criminal activities will continue in the future. In all of the country-specific laws, the judicial capacity to dismember a criminal organization has been greatly enhanced by the enactment of innovative statutes.*

Within these legal frameworks, several countries pioneering anti-mafia policies have also improved their operational capacity for the gathering and

---

*For participation in a criminal association, see the French Criminal Code, Title V, articles 450-1-450-4; the Italian Penal Code, Royal Decree No. 1398 of 19 October 1930, articles 416, "Association for purposes of committing offences", and 416 bis, "Mafia-type association"; and the Spanish Criminal Code, articles 515 and 516, on illicit association.

analysis of complex evidentiary material, over and above the traditional or conventional technique of investigation. Such modern techniques include wire-tapping, controlled delivery, electronic surveillance and testimony obtained from witnesses through offers of immunity or other incentives, coupled with the protection of witnesses. Moreover, international experience in fighting organized crime also shows that law enforcement needs to have the research and analysis capability to support investigations and prosecutions by clearly determining: *(a)* the structure, composition and primary activities of the criminal networks; *(b)* their modus operandi (including production, marketing and financial logistics); *(c)* contacts with both licit and illicit environments; and *(d)* a clear delineation of preventive strategies.

The need for specialized anti-mafia units

International experience shows that specialized units against organized crime at the police and judicial levels or task forces within criminal justice systems are effective tools in fighting organized crime. The establishment of a task force to conduct a complex investigation may take a multi-agency approach where representatives from law enforcement and judicial entities are assigned to specific cases. For example, a task force composed of specialists or skilled investigators from several agencies and prosecutors makes it possible to use a dedicated unit without decimating the available investigative resources from a single organization. The use of team members from other investigative or regulatory agencies often facilitates the gathering of complex evidence. The team concept allows for the clear allocation of assignments and responsibilities among team members and promotes a sense of unity, all necessary for the team's success. In that context, legal advisers or prosecutorial representatives should be included in teams to provide timely legal assistance and leadership in gathering evidentiary material.

The building of specialized units within the criminal justice system is the key to success. The application of team-based management of cases, involving specialized pools of investigators, prosecutors and judges, has been introduced with success in, for example, Chile, Italy and Singapore in order to handle complex criminal cases of asset forfeiture. In some countries, such as Mexico, inter-jurisdictional institutional coordination between federal law enforcement and judicial institutions has proved to be of primary importance in achieving improvements in the investigation and prosecution of cases of organized crime. In the view of the present authors, any national anti-mafia strategy needs to include establishment of a centralized and standardized database on organized criminal groups accessible in real time by law enforcement and judicial officers alike.

Upgrading judicial follow-up

Although higher expenditure on criminal justice does not per se ensure better organized crime and corruption control, it is clear that the criminal justice systems of most developing countries are critically underfunded. The differences in the current and capital levels of spending between developed and developing countries show expanding gaps. For example, developing countries spend an average of $5-$10 on criminal justice per citizen. On the other hand, highly developed economies spend over $165 per citizen on their police, prosecutors and judges. The present analysis showed that many of the low- and middle-income countries in the sample did not even allocate enough resources to keep their criminal justice systems running at a functional level. Besides overall budget increases, reallocations of current budget resources may be warranted in many of these countries where the police receive a disproportionate share of overall funding, while the prosecutorial services and the courts suffer acutely from lack of basic operational resources. Without functioning prosecutorial and judicial systems, law enforcement alone cannot contribute effectively to better conditions for combating complex crimes.

In that framework, courts must monitor and control the progress of cases from filing to disposition by following a group management approach, with first instance court judges and pools of prosecutors jointly managing the cases. Assignment of cases to different management tracks (i.e. express, standard or complex tracks based, among other factors, on the quality and quantity of evidentiary material) can also reduce procedural times and abuse of discretion in case assignments and rulings. Such a system of proactive management must be supported by computerized case-tracking technology, which makes it possible to handle case assignment and to deal with judicial officers' concerns online in real time. Technical personnel and professional staff development must therefore be aimed at adopting more advanced information technologies to support case management.

In countries following best practices, systems to implement forfeiture and financial management of assets have been upgraded in order to include measures that are the most effective in striking at the roots of organized crime. As an incentive to achieve greater operational efficiency, law enforcement agencies could also be allowed to retain the proceeds of asset forfeiture, to be allocated to staff welfare accounts or spent on organizational improvements. (In Chile and Singapore, for example, an autonomous agency handles payment of fines and refunds of bail electronically, with payments credited to the law enforcement departments achieving pre-determined levels of performance.) Previous experience reveals that higher salary levels tend to attract more qualified personnel if subject to strict performance-based indicators, thus making corrupt practices less likely. Yet structural reforms of the judicial system are needed first, including strengthening and modernizing financial management and budgeting while training and developing administrative staff.

In sum, the countries performing best have developed computerized case management processes for police, prosecutors and judges, co-developing multi-agency systems and computerizing court administration. Such reforms have made internal corruption and infiltration by organized crime less likely through the introduction of organizational re-engineering, including elimination of procedural complexity, and through reductions in the abuse of procedural and substantive judicial discretion.

In that connection, legislatures must contribute to empowering the judicial system to take on new and innovative programmes by amending laws, introducing electronic means of handling complex evidence linking many case files, enacting subsidiary legislation for better case management and upgrading judges' salaries.

Involving civil society

The criminal justice systems that are the most effective in fighting organized crime and corruption in the public sector can usually rely on the willingness of citizens to collaborate with the State's law enforcement efforts in an operational way. Building such public confidence and trust in the criminal justice system requires first showing civil society tangible results of successful policy reforms. Moreover, the leadership of the judiciary and law enforcement at the supreme court level, the attorney general, the chief prosecutor and the chief of national police must set good examples by adopting high ethical standards and by establishing strict procedures to ensure that cases are attended to in accordance with due process and are concluded expeditiously. In such a scenario, political will and capacity to execute reforms are a precondition for building public trust and later implementing successful criminal justice policies involving the public.

Reform of criminal justice systems in countries following best practices has not been achieved without the help and support of other institutions.

Political elements are required to foster an independent criminal justice system with the capacity to fight organized crime and public sector corruption.* Recognizing this early on, the countries following best practices have sought to build bridges between their public sectors and civil society stakeholders. Relative success in fighting state captures orchestrated by the Mafia in Palermo, Italy, shows that public information and education campaigns and the fostering of innovative organizational cultures of institutional change within the State have both been catalysts in reducing the pernicious effects of organized crime on corruption in the public sector.**

Civil society actors such as bar associations and law schools can play an important role in the reform process. For example, establishing civil society bodies composed of a panel of lawyers and other members of the public acting as "court watchers" in cases concerning organized crime and corruption in the public sector has been shown to enhance the legitimacy of the judiciary in Costa Rica, Italy and the United States.

Enhancing the independence of the judiciary

Evidence-based results show that a balance between judicial accountability and the independence of judicial institutions from political forces is a necessary condition to achieving success in enforcing laws to fight organized crime and corruption in the public sector. Yet this balance between democratic accountability and institutional independence requires a basic prior consensus among the main political forces in countries [18].

Certainly, it would be naïve to think that constitutional provisions prescribing the separation of powers would be enough to guarantee the judicial independence required for the unbiased and transparent interpretation and enforcement of the law. In fact, such constitutional provisions are not even a necessary condition to attaining judicial independence: countries such as Israel, New Zealand, Sweden and the United Kingdom of Great Britain and Northern Ireland—all countries with high levels of judicial independence coupled with low levels of organized crime and of corruption—do not possess constitutionally entrenched judicial independence.

Examination of international experience shows that the political elements enhancing an independent criminal justice system with the capacity to fight

---

*These elements were all present in the legal and judicial reforms implemented in Chile and Costa Rica [12].

**For more references on using an operational civil society approach supporting law enforcement and judicial efforts, see the work of Leoluca Orlando [18].

organized crime and corruption in the public sector can be identified. For example, the cases of Costa Rica, and to some degree, Chile, show that judicial systems can only enhance their capacity to interpret laws with independence and autonomy when the political concentration of power within the legislative and/or executive branches tends to be relatively balanced such that alternation in power becomes a likely outcome of periodic elections. To some degree, a balance of power among truly competing political forces creates an increased willingness among politicians to give up a good part of their political control of court and prosecutorial decisions in order to avoid mutual assured destruction in subsequent electoral periods when the opposition may take over the reins of power. This sequential "game" between or among political forces operates as a tacit insurance that guarantees increased independence of the criminal justice system from political whims [12].

A framework guiding policy makers during legal and judicial reforms must first identify the main areas where undue pressures are most likely to hamper the State's capacity to adjudicate cases involving organized crime and corruption in the public sector. The identification of such areas must focus on the links between judicial systems and other governmental and non-governmental institutions but also not neglect to review factors hampering independence within the judiciaries themselves. Once the political preconditions for policy reform mentioned above are present, technical initiatives must incorporate best practices. Lessons from case studies show that best practices in enhancing judicial independence of courts and prosecutors include:*

(a) An improved, uniform and comprehensive case management system coupled with transparent and consistent rules for the assignment of cases;

(b) The implementation of uniform and predictable administrative (i.e. personnel- and budget-related) measures founded on rewards and penalties driven by performance-based indicators, with a consequent clarification of the career paths for judicial and law enforcement officers;

(c) Specific reforms of the organizational structure of criminal justice, including the introduction of category-specific organizational roles for judicial, prosecutorial and police personnel in order to secure their own internal independence;

(d) The enhancement of the capacity of the judiciary to review the consistency of its own decisions in court rulings by improving the

---

*These elements of reform aimed at enhancing judicial independence were all present in the legal and judicial reforms implemented in Chile and Costa Rica [12].

effectiveness of judicial (appellate-based) reviews but also by allowing for the monitoring of civil society-based social control mechanisms working hand in hand with the media (e.g. non-governmental organizations such as Court Watch);

　　(e) Governance-related improvements in the links between the political sphere and the judiciary in accordance with the preconditions described above.

Policies within the socio-economic and financial domains

Countries implementing best practice policies in the fight against organized crime and corruption in the public sector have sometimes adopted economic and financial policies that go beyond the legal and judicial measures outlined above. It is clear by now that in order to tackle corruption and organized crime multidimensional measures are required.

In the economic and financial domain, the fight against organized criminal groups includes best practices such as:

　　(a) Reduction of poverty levels and increase in salary levels for public employees in order to hamper the uncontrolled growth of corruption, which tends to increase political instability, which in turn stimulates the penetration of the State by national criminal organizations or, worse, by transnational ones;

　　(b) A reduction in the incidence and dimension of informal markets that provide the economic input and output for organized crime;

　　(c) Improvements in the distribution of income and wealth;

　　(d) Reduction of barriers to the international exchange of goods and services;

　　(e) The adoption and more consistent application of financial regulations, which could be enforced by specialized supervisory state agencies responsible for financial investigations.

In the area of financial regulation, the experience of countries following best practice showed that the capacity of the State to trace, identify, monitor, seize and confiscate financial assets and other types of proceeds of crime, was a key element in any organized crime containment programme. This required a major global infrastructure of legislation not only to address the seizure of proceeds of crime but also for confiscation purposes.

As drug-related issues gain in importance in an increasing number of societies, various efforts have been made to reform legislation to combat laundering of proceeds of crime in different countries, as well as to strengthen the police and prosecutorial involvement in financial investigations (including customs and excise), which increasingly involve tax fraud and terrorist activities. The Financial Action Task Force on Money Laundering, for instance, has begun focusing more on all crime and transnational organized crime, establishing a list of non-cooperative countries and territories in 2000 in order to counteract the slow adoption of standards of the Task Force in some jurisdictions, together with guidelines informing regulated banks the way they should deal with transactions from the listed jurisdictions, introducing more severe sanctions in case of non-compliance.

In that context, it is worth noting that the world's legal landscape has been transformed over the last decade, with an increasing number of countries adopting and enforcing laws permitting or requiring disclosure of assets and mutual legal assistance (although their level of conformity with the standards of the Financial Action Task Force on Money Laundering may vary). Few reputable financial centres now offer bank secrecy as an option. Visible enforcement of financial regulations addressing the proceeds of organized crime has been very modest, however. The lack of operational capacity of police, prosecutors and judges in handling cases involving financial investigations still constitutes an institutional constraint in most countries.

Conclusion

The results of the analyses reported here have shown that levels of organized crime and of corruption in the public sector are determined first and foremost by the quality of core public state institutions, such as the police, prosecution and the courts. That relationship seems to hold for countries at all levels of development. It is also clear that the institutional forces at work in introducing improvements in the legal fight against corruption and organized crime must be held accountable. These are the conditions that foster the "right" institutional environment within which criminal justice can be offered in an unbiased and transparent fashion. Independently from these institutional determinants, high levels of organized crime and corruption are linked to low levels of human development. This result points to the vicious circle of poverty exploited and compounded by organized crime and grand corruption. In extreme cases, dysfunctional state agencies are "captured" by organized crime.

The results of the authors' study confirm the hypothesis that organized crime and corruption prosper in an environment of bad governance. Insufficiencies in the area of economic and financial regulation and poor legal-judicial infrastructures are among the many aspects of governance that appear to be relevant to crime control. This is true for developing countries in general and for countries in post-conflict situations in particular. Examples of countries and territories that gave priority to crime and corruption control in the early stages of development and are now among the most economically successful in their region include Botswana, Hong Kong Special Administrative Region of China, Singapore and Taiwan Province of China. The list of countries and territories with dysfunctional state functions, rampant organized crime and corruption and stagnant economies is by comparison depressingly long [19]. In that context, by strengthening their capacity to prevent and control organized crime, countries can eliminate a major impediment to human development.

Too few developing countries and development experts seem to appreciate fully the far-reaching impact of a functioning criminal justice system. Unlike conventional crime, which seems to be controlled largely by structural root causes outside the sphere of short- or medium-term influence of the State [20-21], organized crime and corruption in the public sector seem more susceptible to state intervention. This finding has important implications for both crime control and development policies. Human development prospects are conditional on the effective control of organized crime and corruption through law enforcement and the rule of law. This being the case, the required investment in law enforcement and prosecutorial and judicial systems in developing countries aimed at enhancing capacity to combat organized crime is small compared with the investments needed to bring physical infrastructure up to international standards.

References

1. Louise I. Shelley, "Transnational organized crime: an imminent threat to the nation-state?", *Journal of International Affairs*, vol. 48, No. 2 (winter 1995), pp. 463-489.

2. Samuel Gonzalez-Ruiz and Edgardo Buscaglia, "How to design a national strategy against organized crime in the framework of the United Nations' Palermo convention", *The Fight against Organized Crime* (Lima, United Nations International Drug Control Programme, 2002), pp. 23-26.

3. World Economic Forum, "Organized crime imposes cost on businesses", *The Global Competitiveness Report 2002-2003* (New York, Oxford University Press, 2003).

4. Jan van Dijk and Sami Nevala, "Intercorrelations of crime: results of an analysis of the correlations between indices of different types of conventional and non-conventional crime", *Crime Victimization in Comparative Perspective*, Paul Nieuwbeerta, ed. (The Hague, Boom Juridische Uitgevers, 2002), pp. 182-193.

5. Jan van Dijk, Mark Shaw and Edgardo Buscaglia, "The TOC Convention and the need for comparative research: some illustrations from the work of the UN Centre for International Crime Prevention", *The Containment of Transnational Organized Crime*, Hans-Jörg Albrecht and Cyrille Fijnaut, eds. (Freiburg, Germany, edition iuscrim, 2002, pp. 31-54).

6. Curtis Milhaupt and Mark West "The dark side of private ordering: an institutional and empirical analysis of organized crime", *University of Chicago Law Review*, vol. 67, No. 1 (winter 2000).

7. Jeff Huther and Anwar Shah, *Anti-Corruption Policies and Programs: a Framework for Evaluation*, Working Paper No. 2501 (Washington, D.C., World Bank, 2001).

8. Anna Alvazzi del Frate, "The voice of victims of crime: estimating the true level of conventional crime", *Forum on Crime and Society*, vol. 3, Nos. 1-2 (2003).

9. *EUROSHORE: Protecting the EU Financial System from the Exploitation Of Financial Centres and Offshore Facilities by Organized Crime* (Trento, Italy, University of Trento, 2000).

10. Edgardo Buscaglia, "Judicial corruption in developing countries: its causes and economic consequences", *Essays in Public Policy* (Stanford University, Hoover Institution Press, 2000), pp. 24-29.

11. Edgardo Buscaglia, "Judicial corruption in Latin America", *Essays in Law and Economics* (Amsterdam, Kluwer, 1997).

12. Florencio Lopez-de-Silanes and others, "The regulation of entry", *Quarterly Journal of Economics*, vol. 117, No. 1 (February 2002), pp. 1-37.

13. P. C. van Duyne, "Will 'Caligula' go transparent? Corruption in acts and attitudes", *Forum on Crime and Society*, vol. 1, No. 2 (2001), pp. 73-98.

14. Daniel Treisman, "Decentralization and the quality of government", unpublished article.

15. Susan Rose-Ackerman and Jana Kunicova, "Electoral rules as constraints on corruption", Yale University, 2001.

16. Daniel Kaufmann, Aart Kraay and Pablo Zoido-Lobatón, *Governance Matters*, Working Paper No. 2196 (Washington, D.C., World Bank, 1999).

17. Alberto Vannucci, "Corruption, political parties, and political protection", *EUI working papers of the Robert Schuman Centre* (Florence, Italy, European University Institute, 2000).

18. Leoluca Orlando, *Fighting the Mafia and Reviewing Sicilian Culture* (San Francisco, California, Encounter Books, 2003).

19. *World Bank Group work in low-income countries under stress: a task force report* (Washington, D.C., World Bank, 2002).

20. Jan van Dijk, "The experience of crime and justice", *Global Report on Crime and Justice* (New York, Oxford University Press, 1999), pp. 25-42.

21. Pablo Fajnzylber, Daniel Lederman and Norman Loayza, "Inequality and violent crime", *Journal of Law and Economics*, vol. XLV, No. 1 (2002).

DETERMINING TRENDS IN GLOBAL CRIME AND JUSTICE: AN OVERVIEW OF RESULTS FROM THE UNITED NATIONS SURVEYS OF CRIME TRENDS AND OPERATIONS OF CRIMINAL JUSTICE SYSTEMS

by Mark Shaw,* Jan van Dijk** and Wolfgang Rhomberg***

Abstract

Effectively measuring comparative developments in crime and justice trends from a global perspective remains a key challenge for international policy makers. The ability to compare crime levels across countries enables policy makers to determine where interventions should occur and improves understanding of the key causes of crime in different societies across the globe. Nevertheless, there are significant challenges to comparative work in the field of criminal justice, not least of which is the ability to quantify accurately levels of crime across countries. Taking into account the methodological weaknesses of using cross-country data sources, the present article provides conclusions obtained by analysing the large amount of data available from the various United Nations surveys of crime trends and operations of criminal justice systems.

*"Not everything that can be counted, counts.
And not everything that counts can be counted."* Albert Einstein

INTRODUCTION

The United Nations Survey of Crime Trends and Operations of Criminal Justice Systems is one of the few sources of data on Government-reported levels of crime worldwide [1].**** The United Nations Survey of Crime Trends has been used by a number of academic analysts and in a series

---

*Crime Prevention and Criminal Justice Officer, United Nations Office on Drugs and Crime.
**Officer-in-Charge, Human Security Branch, United Nations Office on Drugs and Crime.
***Database Analyst, United Nations Office on Drugs and Crime.
****The United Nations Survey of Crime Trends and Operations of Criminal Justice Systems is not, however, the only source of international criminal justice statistics. The International Criminal Police Organization (Interpol) also publishes a yearly list of international reported crime statistics (available at www.interpol.int/Public/Statistics/ICS/Default.asp), as does the Home Office of the United Kingdom of Great Britain and Northern Ireland: see *International Comparisons of Criminal Justice Statistics* 2000 [1].

of studies carried out by the World Bank [2-3].* The Survey has been conducted seven times, beginning with the period 1970-1975. For the Seventh United Nations Survey of Crime Trends and Operations of Criminal Justice Systems, covering the period 1998-2000, data were received from 82 countries. The Survey consists of 518 variables, covering all manner of information, from figures on reported crime to the numbers of police officers, prosecutors, magistrates, judges and correctional officials working in a country. The database is becoming increasingly valuable to international and national policy makers in the field of criminal justice. The Survey is unique in terms of the number of participating countries, the number of times it has been conducted and the number of variables that are surveyed.

The main goal of the United Nations Survey of Crime Trends is to collect data on the incidence of reported crime and the operations of criminal justice systems with a view to improving the analysis and dissemination of the information globally. The results provide an overview of trends and the interrelationships of various parts of the criminal justice system so as to promote informed decision-making in administration, both nationally and internationally. By their nature, the conclusions that can be drawn from the survey data, unless detailed analysis on a country-per-country basis is carried out, must be considered as high-level overviews of trends.

The present article contains a short review of the methodological difficulties of cross-country comparisons, including a comparison of international crime data from two sources. It also provides a comparative overview of overall reported crime levels, as well as some insight into trends and comparisons in respect of two types of crime, homicide and robbery. In addition, data are presented in respect of various measures of both criminal justice performance and resource allocation. In conclusion, suggestions as to the possible future organization of the United Nations Survey of Crime Trends are made.

The hazards of cross-country comparison

It is important to preface a presentation on international comparative crime data with a number of provisos about the overall reliability of the exercise.

---

*See, for example, the article by Pablo Fajnzylber, Daniel Lederman and Norman Loayza, entitled "Inequality and violent crime" [2]. A more recent comprehensive review of the data from the United Nations Survey of Crime Trends can be found in *Global Report on Crime and Justice* [3].

Comparing crime statistics from different jurisdictions is a hazardous undertaking. For a start, the crime category for which any incidents are recorded relies on the legal definition of that type of crime in a particular country. Should the definition differ across countries, and indeed this is often the case, comparisons will not, in fact, be made of the same type of crime. This is particularly true in the case of crimes that require some discretion from a police officer or other relevant authority when they are identified. For example, the definitional difference between serious or common assault in different legal jurisdictions may be different, and this will be reflected in the total number of incidents recorded.

Over and above such definitional issues, different countries have been shown to have different levels of reporting of criminal incidents [4]. This relates closely to the level of development of a society, which is most clearly reflected in the accessibility of the police. Thus, factors such as the number of police stations or telephones in a country affect reporting levels. The level of insurance coverage in a community is also a key indicator of the likelihood of citizens approaching the police, as their claim for compensation may require prior notification of the police. In addition, in countries where the police are or have been mistrusted by the population, most specifically during periods of authoritarian rule, reporting levels are likely to be lower than in countries where the police are regarded as important members of the community.

It should also be noted that comparing crime data from societies that are fundamentally different might ignore key issues that affect levels of reporting. For example, in some societies, social norms may make it almost impossible for women to report cases of rape or sexual abuse, while in others, women are encouraged to come forward. The impact on any attempt to compare crime levels accurately is obvious [5].*

These factors, while alerting the reader to the potential pitfalls of comparisons, apply more to some types of crime than others. In selected cases, most notably homicide, cross-country comparisons are more reliable, although they may still be subject to the drawbacks outlined above. In the case of some categories of violent crime, such as rape and assault, cross-country comparisons may simply be unreliable and misleading, due to a combination of definitional and reporting problems.

---

*A detailed overview of the potential pitfalls of cross-country data comparison can be found in *Global Report on Crime and Justice* [5].

In addition to those issues, even when crime statistics are available, there may be discrepancies in the data when they are drawn from different sources. That is illustrated by comparing the homicide figures for one year (1999) of the United Nations Survey of Crime Trends and Operations of Criminal Justice Systems with those of the International Criminal Police Organization (Interpol).* In only a few cases were the figures for the same countries identical in each database. The Interpol database generally reflected a greater number of recorded homicides. In a limited number of cases, the United Nations Survey of Crime Trends reflected higher totals than the Interpol database, but generally by a lower margin.

One possible explanation for the divergence is that the data were obtained through different sources. In the case of Interpol, they are usually obtained directly from police sources, while the United Nations Survey of Crime Trends collects figures through the Statistics Division of the United Nations Secretariat, directly from the statistical authorities or the department of justice in each country. In addition, the United Nations Survey of Crime Trends generally has a longer time lag than does Interpol before the data are requested. That may mean that by the time data are reported in the United Nations Survey of Crime Trends, countries have had a greater opportunity to clean and review their figures and have eliminated cases that had been incorrectly recorded as homicides.

What is interesting, apart from the discrepancies themselves, is the comparatively small number of countries that report to both Interpol and the United Nations Survey of Crime Trends. Yet, despite this, each database contains statistics for over 100 countries. While the comparison has been completed for only one type of crime and one year, it does suggest that considerably more data may be available than have been recorded by either Interpol or the United Nations Office on Drugs and Crime.

Given the problems, the question of why there is continued interest at the United Nations Office on Drugs and Crime in bringing together a wealth of statistical data on criminal justice issues from a variety of jurisdictions may legitimately be asked. First, it should be emphasized that the main purpose of the United Nations Survey of Crime Trends is not to measure the exact amount of crime that exists in the world or to compare levels of crime across countries, but rather to provide an accounting of crimes processed by the various components of the criminal justice system.

---

*It should be noted that the Interpol database includes only recorded crime figures, whereas that of the United Nations Survey of Crime Trends and Operations of Criminal Justice Systems also includes information on the performance of criminal justice systems.

Second, trends in levels of crime recorded by the police are of interest as a rough indication of trends in actual levels of crime, since reporting and recording patterns can be assumed to be relatively stable over time. It may, in short, not be possible to conclude from official figures on crime that the level of crime in country A is higher than in country B. Long-term trends in such figures do, however, under normal circumstances, reflect trends in the actual number of crimes committed. For that reason, the value of such a survey is enhanced with an increasing number of sweeps, allowing the emergence of a picture of trends in individual societies.

The present article seeks therefore to provide some insight into the possibility of identifying overall trends in reported crime, as well as trends in the operations of criminal justice systems, such as conviction rates. While the administration of the United Nations Survey of Crime Trends stretches back to the early 1970s, data referred to in the present article are from the last five surveys (up to and including the Seventh Survey), covering the period 1980-2000.

Global crime trends and comparisons

When measuring crime trends over time, it is essential to ensure that the periods analysed are long enough. Crime trends measured over too short a period provide little indication of overall developments and may, in fact, by illustrating random increases or decreases, be misleading. While the data from the various United Nations surveys of crime trends stretches back three decades, their degree of reliability, the number of responses from countries and the compatibility between the various questionnaires make it difficult to use the data to illustrate trends over such long periods of time. For many crime categories, however, trends from 1980 to 2000 can be determined, providing a 20-year review of developments.

The section below contains a comparative review of three data sets from the United Nations survey of crime trends.

The first data set relates to comparison of overall reported crime rates across countries. Although, for the reasons given above, the levels of overall crime do not in any reliable way reflect actual levels of crime, long-term trends in recorded crime provide a useful point of departure for a comparative analysis of regional crime problems [1].

The second data set is for homicides. Comparing levels of homicide is the most common comparative measure of crime in countries, given what are generally regarded to be higher levels of reliability of the available data. In cases where a murder has occurred, either the incident is reported to the police or the authorities stumble upon the victim's remains. In all the countries providing data for the survey, homicide is the crime most likely to be reported and/or recorded. On this basis, homicide levels from different countries provide a relatively reliable source of comparison. In addition, homicide is generally regarded as a good proxy for broader levels of violent crime.

The third data set is for robbery. While data on robbery are unlikely to be as accurate for the purpose of cross-country comparisons as those for homicide, they are likely to be more reliable than data on lesser property crimes such as theft. That is because robberies are property crimes perpetrated with the use of violence or the threat thereof; consequently, their victims have a double incentive to report the crime, namely, the physical and psychological trauma caused by the use of violence and the loss of property [2].* In developing countries, in particular, robbery is an important crime, not only because it causes injury and property loss to the victim, but also because it raises the general level of fear of crime. Nevertheless, it must be conceded that the crime of robbery in most countries includes a wide purview of offences, from street mugging to bank robberies, and country comparisons are fraught with problems. In addition, in the case of some crimes that are classified as robbery, such as bank robberies or car hijackings, high levels of such crimes may be an indicator of the activities of organized criminal groups [6].** Data in respect of each of these three data sets, for overall crime levels, homicide and robbery rates, are presented below.

Overall recorded crime trends since 1980

To provide a global review of the development of reported crime trends since 1980, the comparative figures for total recorded crime have been graphed over time, with the trends for selected regions being presented. Total recorded crime for all the countries on which the United Nations surveys of crime trends have yielded data shows a steady increase from

---

*This is an argument also made by Fajnzylber, Lederman and Loayza [2] in a cross-country comparison that sought to determine the links between levels of crime and economic inequality.

**This is the case, for example, in South Africa, where the problem of car hijacking in some cities is closely related to the activities of criminal gangs. Since car hijackings constitute a significant proportion of all robbery rates, almost always involve the use of firearms and perpetrated by criminal gangs, their overall number provides a good indication of the strength of organized crime in an area.

2,300 incidents per 100,000 people in 1980 to just over 3,000 in 2000. Worldwide, problems of crime have become worse over the past two decades.

Increases in the overall volume of recorded crime are most notable in the case of Latin America and the Caribbean and closely mirror the global trend. At a lower level, similar upward trends are present for Eastern Europe and the Commonwealth of Independent States, South-East Asia and the Pacific, as well as the Arab States. The data for sub-Saharan Africa shows a less clear trend, with notable increases in the early 1990s being followed by a marked decline. A detailed examination of the data for Africa, however, suggests that the overall trend is not reliable, given the small number of States that provide crime data through the United Nations surveys of crime trends. The data for those regions have been combined and are reflected in figure I as the trend for "selected regions".

The most striking declines in overall levels of recorded crime have occurred in North America; since the early 1990s, the total volume of crime per 100,000 citizens has declined steadily in both Canada and the United States of America, although the decline was more pronounced in the United States. Such a trend has been noted before and the data presented in figure I are consistent with early findings [7-9] and data from other sources.*

The data for the European Union present a less clear picture. A close examination of the data shows that in some countries within the European Union there has been a decline in the overall crime level. The overall trend, having increased noticeably in the early 1980s, has stabilized at just over 6,000 cases per 100,000 inhabitants. Data for the late 1990s do, however, suggest an increase more recently. What is, perhaps, most remarkable is that the overall volumes of crime recorded in the European Union countries surpassed those for North America in the late 1990s, as confirmed by other sources; overall levels of crime are no longer necessarily higher in the United States than in the European Union [4].

While it is not clear why crime levels in North America and some parts of the European Union have been declining, one possible explanation is that the sustained focus on crime countermeasures taken by both the private and public sectors over the period under review has begun to reap dividends. Such an explanation applies more clearly to North America, in particular, the United States, than it does to the European Union, which, while not showing any dramatic increase over the 20-year period, has also

---

*The declines in levels of crime in North America and some European countries have been confirmed by evidence from the International Crime Victim Survey.

not shown any dramatic decline. Again, it should be pointed out that presenting the data for the European Union as a single trend masks declines in crimes in some countries and increases in others [1].*

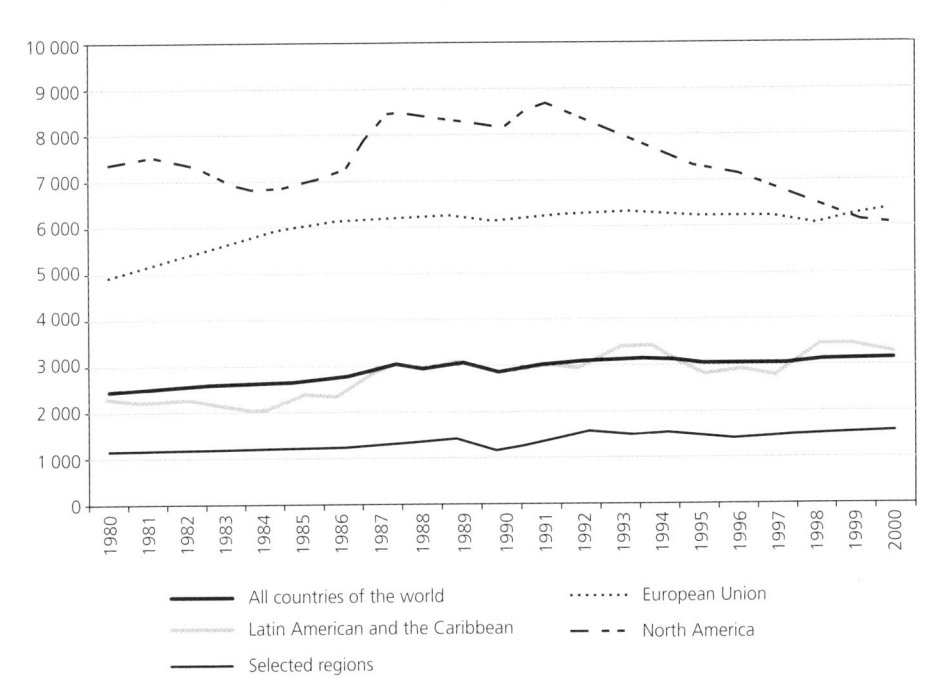

Figure I. Total recorded crime trends per 100,000 population in selected regions of the world

―――― All countries of the world ········ European Union
―――― Latin American and the Caribbean ― ― ― North America
―――― Selected regions

Source: United Nations Office on Drugs and Crime.

Despite these decreases, overall levels of recorded crime in all regions of the world are still significantly lower than those in the high-income countries of North America and the European Union. That is presumably because the propensity to report crimes in many regions elsewhere in the world is much lower. The results of the International Crime Victim Survey, discussed in the present issue of *Forum* [4], confirm this assumption. Indeed, it is possible to assume that in most middle- and low-income countries the crimes that are reported are, on average, much more serious than those in high-income countries. This assumption is reinforced by an analysis of the data for both middle- and low-income countries, which shows that in developing countries the proportion of violent crimes is higher

---

*Barclay and Tavares [1] provide a more detailed discussion and presentation of the available data, noting an increase of 1 per cent in recorded crime for the European Union for the period 1996-2000.

than property crimes.* Thus, while the overall quality of official crime data in middle- and low-income countries may be lower than in high-income countries, those crimes that are reported are, on average, of a more serious nature, with a greater proportion involving violence. It should also be noted that increased economic development (reflected, for example, by the number of motor vehicles) and changes in technology (such as greater use of computers, mobile telephones, and so forth) have expanded and are likely to continue to expand opportunities for crime in middle-income countries, in particular, as well as opportunities to report such crimes to the police. Those countries are likely to show further increases in recorded crime in the years to come, reflecting an upward trend in the level of crime.

Comparative rates of homicide

Figure II shows homicide rates in those countries that have reported data to the United Nations surveys of crime trends. The data provided show a similar ordering of countries to the Interpol data, with Colombia and South Africa showing the highest level of recorded homicide of those countries which submitted data. The graph represents average homicide rates over a 20-year period, 1980-2000.

The data from the United Nations surveys of crime trends suggest that the majority of European Union member and accession States (with the exception of Estonia, Latvia and Lithuania) fall below the global average. The most prominent exception among developed countries is the United States, which falls just above the global average. Homicide rates tend to be higher in developing countries, in particular in middle-income and developing countries that have experienced either sustained periods of civil conflict or political transition, such as Colombia, the Russian Federation and South Africa.

Broad generalizations about crime levels in the developed and developing world must, however, be made with care. In a number of cases, such as Botswana, which, according to data from the United Nations Survey of Crime Trends, has the lowest level of recorded homicide in the world, developing countries fall below the global average. All the countries considered to have a high level of human development, however, fall below the global homicide average, with the prominent exception of the United States. And, all the countries which show serious levels of homicide, above 10 per 100,000 inhabitants are either middle-income (Mexico, Russian Federation, South Africa) or developing countries.

---

*The assumption is based on an analysis of three violent crimes (homicide, serious assault and assault) and two property crimes (burglary and theft).

Figure II. Average homicides per 100,000 inhabitants,

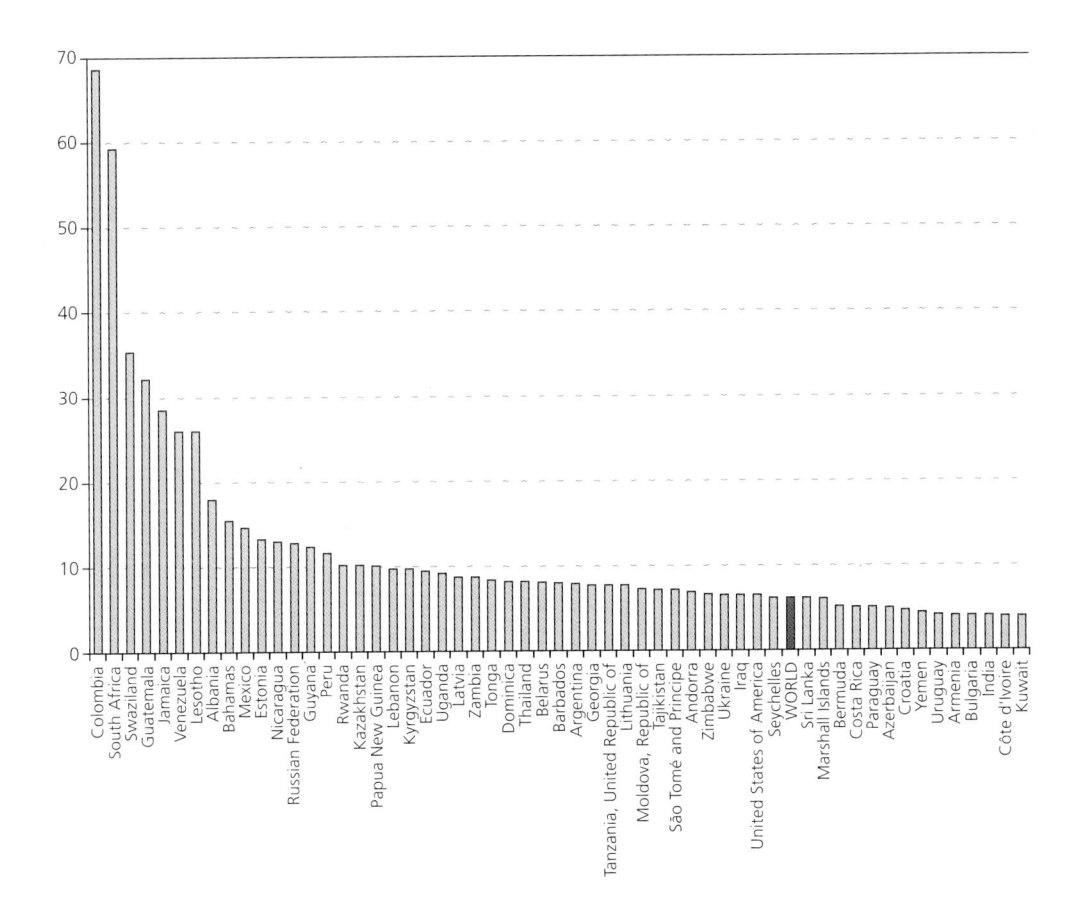

Source: United Nations Office on Drugs and Crime.
[a]SAR = Special Administrative Region.

selected countries and areas, 1980-2000

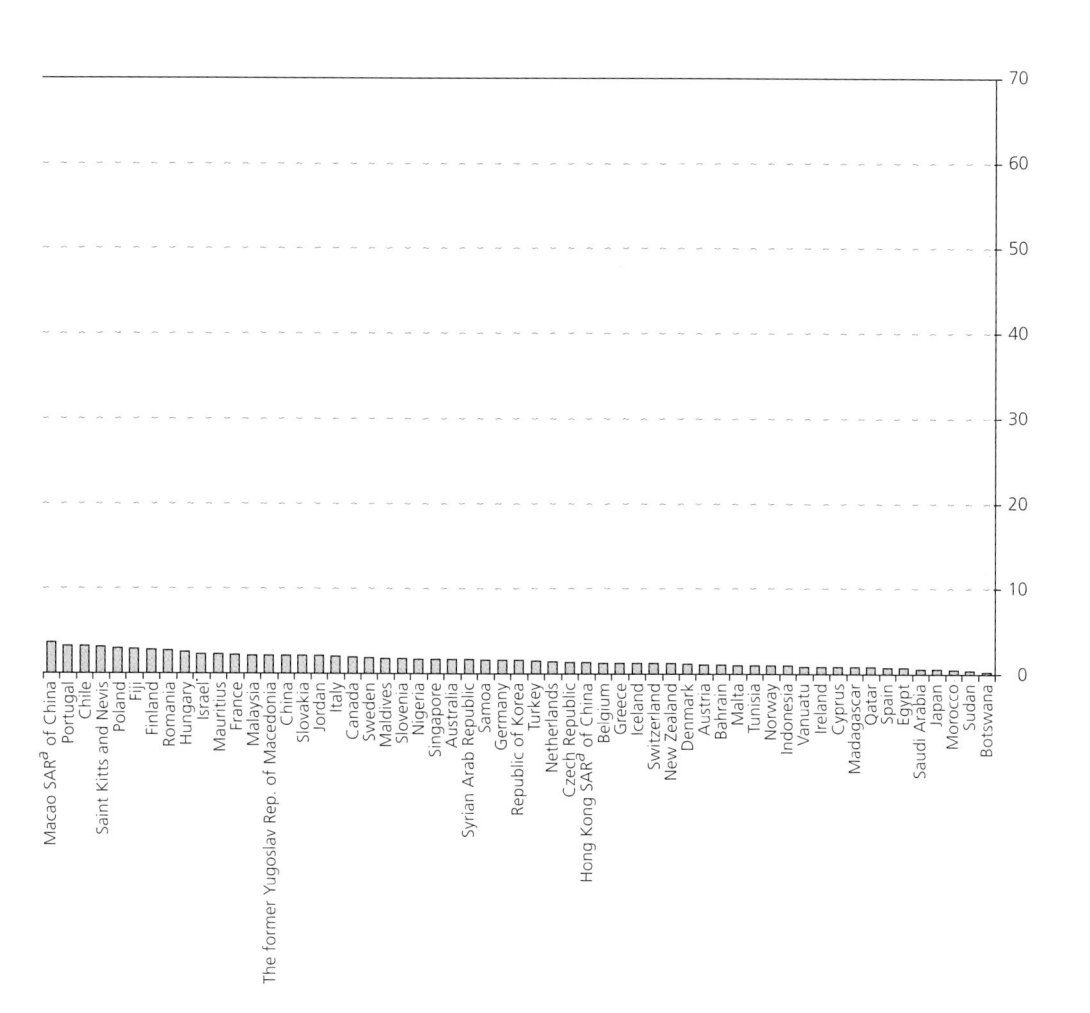

The average homicide rate in those countries which reported data to the survey is 7 homicides per 100,000 inhabitants. Of interest here is that the World Health Organization (WHO) estimates the global homicide rate in the late 1990s to be about 8.8 per 100,000 inhabitants [10]. On average, over a 16-year period, the WHO research can be shown to have recorded 15 per cent more homicide cases than the United Nations surveys of crime trends. The higher global average of WHO probably reflects two factors. First, WHO mortality studies cover a larger number of developing countries where homicides are higher; indeed, the WHO figures show that suicides are considerably more common than homicides in developed countries, with the opposite being the case in developing countries. Second, the WHO figures are generally based on hospital surveys of the cause of death. Police-reported data, as reflected in the United Nations surveys of crime trends, often only reflect the first assessment of the crime as a homicide. Thus, the death of an injured person who is taken to hospital and dies there later may be recorded as a homicide by WHO, but as an attempted murder or serious assault by the police. Hospitals may also wrongly, from a legal perspective, clarify cases of assault resulting in death as homicide.

A more detailed examination of the WHO data for homicide, in comparison with those of the United Nations surveys of crime trends, highlights another and critical reason for the difference. The WHO data, as has already been pointed out, are based on hospital-based surveys and so, in fact, may provide a useful insight into the proportion of cases of homicide that actually appear in the reported police statistics in the first place. This is illustrated in figure III, which shows the differences between the homicide data of WHO and those of the United Nations surveys of crime trends compared over a 16-year period in high-, medium- and low-income countries.

Figure III shows that in high-income countries the data reported to WHO and the United Nations surveys of crime trends over a 16-year period differ by only 2 per cent, with the United Nations surveys of crime trends reporting, in effect, 2 per cent more cases of homicide. In middle- and low-income countries, however, the WHO data show significantly more cases of homicide, 18 and 45 per cent respectively. Given that the two sets of data come from different sources, the exercise serves as a useful cross-check. It can be assumed from the data that in middle- and low-income countries, even for a crime such as homicide that is regarded as well-reported, there are significant levels of under-reporting to or under-recording by the police.

Figure III. Percentage of homicides reported by the World Health Organization as compared to those reported by the United Nations surveys of crime trends and operations of criminal justice systems, 1986-2000

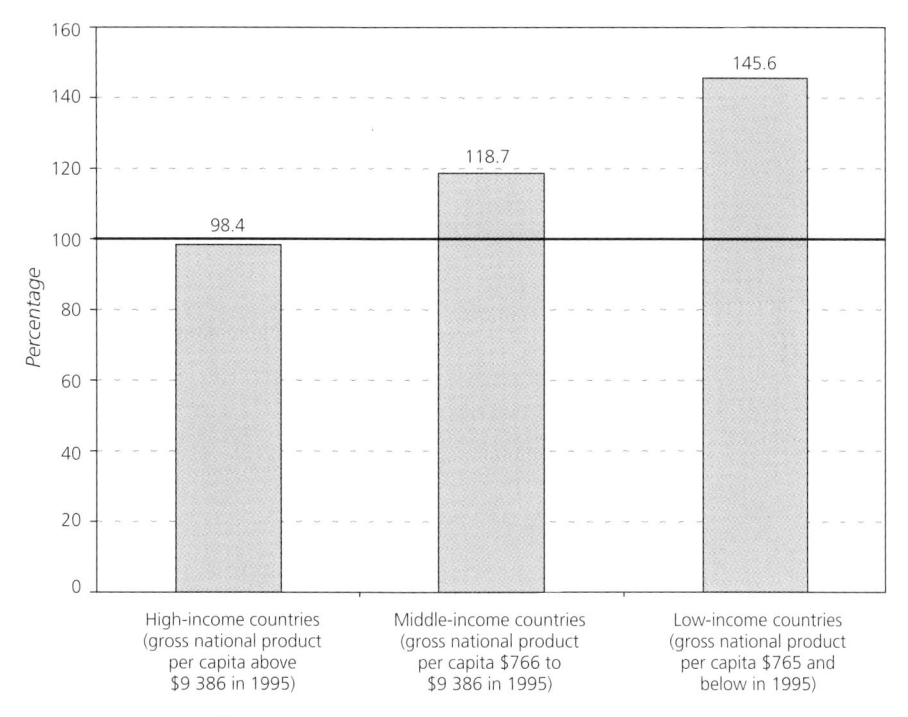

(United Nations surveys = 100 per cent)

Category	Percentage
High-income countries (gross national product per capita above $9 386 in 1995)	98.4
Middle-income countries (gross national product per capita $766 to $9 386 in 1995)	118.7
Low-income countries (gross national product per capita $765 and below in 1995)	145.6

Source: United Nations Office on Drugs and Crime.

Regional homicide trends

The available data for Latin America and the Caribbean show extraordinarily high levels of homicide, at around 25 cases per 100,000 inhabitants, across the reporting period (see figure IV). The overall trend is relatively consistent, although there is a noticeable increase in the early 1990s (above 25 incidents per 100,000 inhabitants), followed by some declines. The late 1990s again suggests another increase in recorded cases.

The available data for sub-Saharan Africa also show comparatively high levels of homicide: between 17 and 20 incidents per 100,000 inhabitants. There is no clear overall trend, but there does appear to be a steady decline from the mid-1990s onwards.

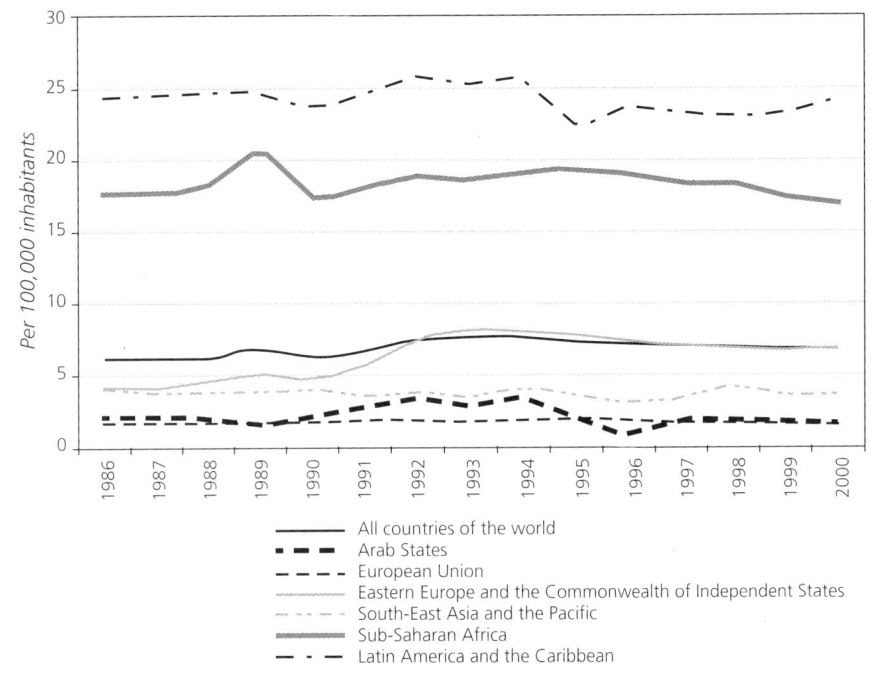

Figure IV. Rates of homicides, 1986-2000: selected regional trends

———— All countries of the world
■ ■ ■ Arab States
- - - - European Union
~~~~~ Eastern Europe and the Commonwealth of Independent States
- - - - South-East Asia and the Pacific
▓▓▓▓ Sub-Saharan Africa
— · — Latin America and the Caribbean

Source: United Nations Office on Drugs and Crime.

The overall trend for the European Union shows comparatively low levels of homicide, under three incidents per 100,000 inhabitants, with a slight decline being noted in the number of cases being recorded at the end of the 1990s. The data for the European Union should be considered accurate, as a large number of countries report statistics with a high level of reliability. Data for North America were not included in the graph as only Canada had consistently provided data across the reporting period. The homicide figures for Canada mirror those of the European Union and, as stated earlier, United States homicide rates, though declining, are at an incomparably higher level than those for the European Union.

Of all the regions under consideration, data from Eastern Europe and the Commonwealth of Independent States show the clearest increases across the reporting period. While in the mid-1980s homicide rates in the region were recorded at under five incidents per 100,000 inhabitants, increases occurred from the late 1980s into the early 1990s, peaking during 1993 and 1994 at approximately eight incidents per 100,000 inhabitants, and thereafter showed slight declines.

The available data for South-East Asia and the Pacific, excluding some countries that have not reported, show a relatively consistent trend, with between three and four homicides per 100,000 inhabitants being reported.

Data for the Arab States, while always remaining below four incidents per 100,000 people, show greater fluctuations across the reporting period. From 1986 to 1990, the level of homicide in that region was comparable to that of the European Union and Canada. The number of cases reported increased during the late 1980s and early 1990s, then declined to previous levels.

The global rate of homicide since the early 1980s

The increase in the rate of homicide between 1991 and 1995 is in line with significant increases in homicide in a number of countries that were undergoing transitions from authoritarian rule to democracy during that period. This is reflected in the data for Eastern Europe and the Commonwealth of Independent States, to some extent in the data for Latin America, as well as in those for specific countries such as South Africa [11-12]. Higher levels of homicide were recorded in the early 1990s, with a slight decline occurring thereafter.

Global reported homicide levels, as reported to the United Nations surveys of crime trends over a 16-year period, have been remarkably stable, showing only a slight increase over the whole reporting period.

Comparative trends in robbery

Figure V shows robbery trends over a 20-year period between 1980 and 2000, for both the global average and various regions. It should be emphasized at the outset that an examination of robbery data on a country-by-country basis is unlikely to yield reliable conclusions. Nevertheless, some analysis of the available regional trends seems warranted.

The global rate for robbery suggests a relatively steady upward trend from 1980 to 2000, from just under 40 incidents per 100,000 inhabitants to just over 60. The overall trend for the European Union closely mirrors this, although beginning with lower levels of robbery in 1980.

As in the case of overall volumes of crime, North America showed dramatic declines from the early 1990s in recorded cases of robbery, from just under

200 incidents per 100,000 inhabitants to around 120 incidents. This decline is all the more remarkable given the earlier increases in robbery rates that had occurred from the mid-1980s to the early 1990s. It should be noted that robbery rates for North America, despite their declines, were much higher throughout the recording period than those of the European Union.

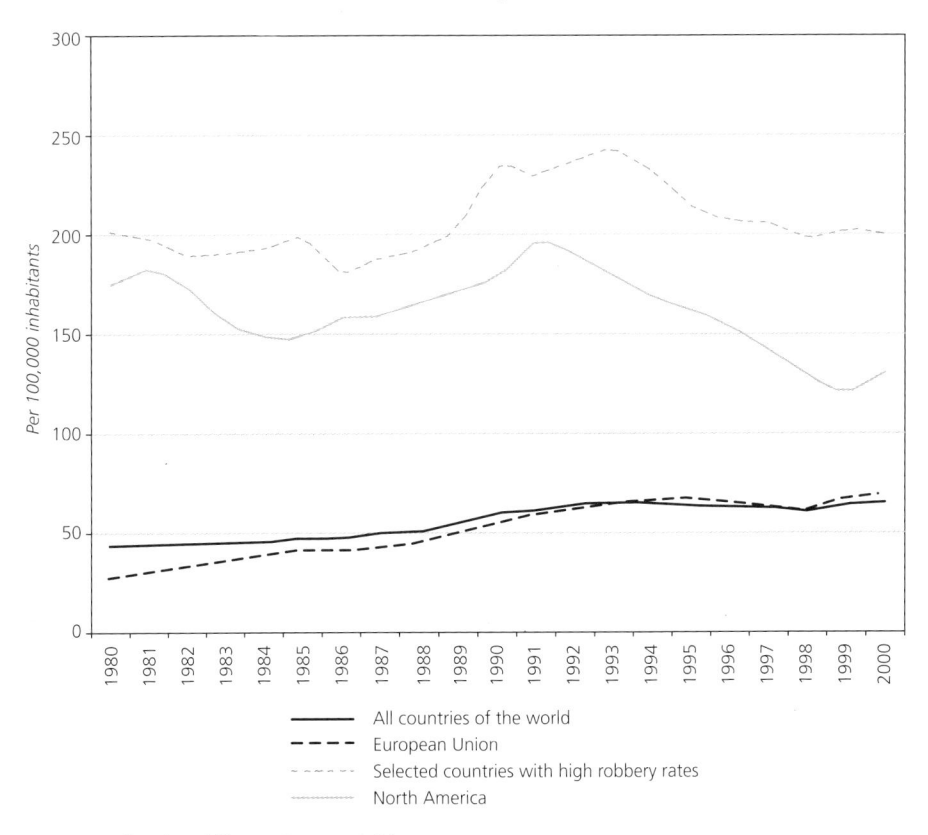

Figure V. Trends in reported robbery per 100,000 inhabitants, selected regions

——— All countries of the world
- - - - European Union
- - - - - Selected countries with high robbery rates
············ North America

Source: United Nations Office on Drugs and Crime.

Robbery rates for other regions of the world were insignificant or the data were too patchy for clear conclusions to be drawn. Nevertheless, robbery remains a serious concern in a number of middle-income and developing societies, the data for which have been isolated and presented in figure V;*

---

*This reflects the available data for countries that have levels of robbery above 100 incidents per 100,000 inhabitants and includes data for Argentina, Costa Rica, Ecuador, Jamaica, Peru, the Russian Federation, Swaziland and Zimbabwe.

the line for selected countries with high robbery rates shows overall increases in robbery until the mid-1990s, followed by significant declines. Of interest is the "hump" in the trend line between 1988 and 1995; that was a period of extraordinarily high robbery rates in those countries at the time (being on average close to 250 incidents per 100,000 inhabitants, coinciding with a period of significant economic, political and social change in a number of those States).

A more detailed look at the statistics and the countries that have provided them, largely those in Eastern Europe and Latin America, as well as South Africa, suggests that in almost all cases transition to democracy was accompanied by increases in both homicides and violent property crimes such as robbery. In all cases levels of violent robbery are of great concern to Governments and citizens [13]. The development of violent forms of robbery must be viewed as an issue of particular concern in countries attempting to consolidate hard-won democracies in the context of economic instability.

Criminal justice performance

The United Nations Survey of Crime Trends and Operations of Criminal Justice Systems also collects information around a series of indicators of the performance of criminal justice systems. Again, various definitional and other problems make the process of comparison difficult. Nevertheless, in respect of a number of variables it is possible to draw some important conclusions. For the purpose of the present article, data on a number of specific issues have been used: the success that various systems report on arresting, prosecuting and convicting offenders; the numbers of personnel working within the criminal justice systems; and, finally, the available budgets, including the allocation of resources between various components of the criminal justice system.

Attrition rates

Data provided by the United Nations Survey of Crime Trends can be used to some extent to compare the effectiveness of criminal justice systems. One way of measuring their effectiveness is to examine the "attrition rates" of selected types of crime as they proceed through the system. In effect, this measure reflects which proportion of cases entering the system are duly resolved, closed or dispensed with by criminal justice agencies. Levels of attrition can be measured at a number of points within a criminal justice system. For example, one could be to examine how many police-recorded cases of a serious crime are actually prosecuted. Another could be to examine how many recorded or prosecuted cases result in a conviction.* Such a comparison provides a broad indication of the overall efficiency of the criminal justice system.

Figures VI and VII show various regional comparisons in respect of the proportion of cases where a conviction was obtained as compared to the number of cases recorded. In each case, the graphs illustrate the number of recorded crimes as a ratio of the number of convictions obtained. The data cover the period 1990-2000 for the crimes of homicide and robbery.**

In respect of the proportion of convictions obtained for police-recorded homicides (figure VI), the data show sub-Saharan Africa to be in a poor position, with a conviction being obtained in only one of every 18 cases recorded by the police. In South-East Asia and the Pacific, a conviction is obtained on average in about one in every nine recorded cases. Of interest here is the case of North America, where the conviction rate is low and below the global average compared to the number of recorded cases. One possible explanation is the relatively high acquittal rate for homicide prosecutions. By contrast, in Latin America, where fewer prosecutions are initiated, the ones that do occur are more likely to result in a conviction.***

The attrition rates for robbery show a slightly different picture. Sub-Saharan Africa could not be included in figure VII as there were insufficient data to draw reliable conclusions in respect of convictions. Nevertheless, the available data for the number of prosecutions initiated show the position in Africa to be serious. On average, only one in every 40 cases of reported robbery resulted in a prosecution for the period 1990-2000. In respect of robbery convictions and as shown in figure VII, South-East Asia and the Pacific shows the most serious position, with only one conviction for every 35 cases of robbery recorded. This is followed by Latin America and the

---

*Such indicators can provide only a rough measure of success as they do not generally measure the same series of actual cases (this is the case with the United Nations Survey of Crime Trends). This is because court systems generally take a long time to process cases and therefore the number of reported incidents in any given year, measured against the number of prosecutions under way or convictions achieved in that year, do not measure the same series of cases against each other.

**In some cases, data on selected regions could not be included because data quality was inadequate.

***The ratio for the number of recorded homicides as compared to the number of homicide prosecutions for North America is approximately 2:1, while for Latin America it is 3:1.

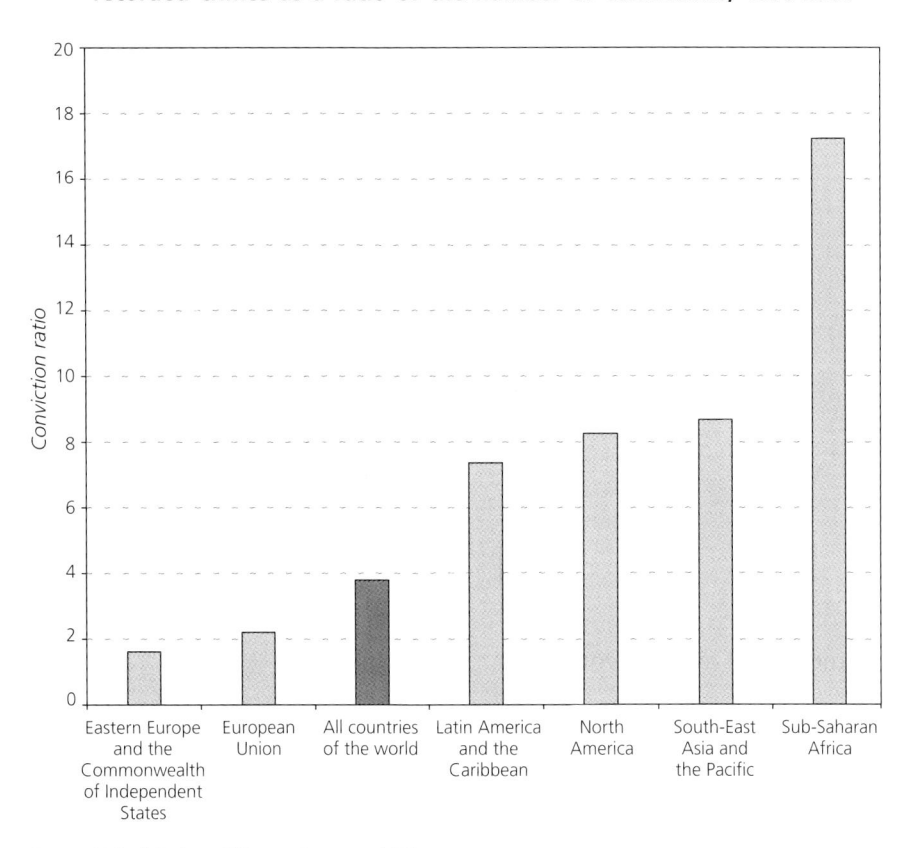

Figure VI. Comparative regional attrition rates for homicide: the number of recorded crimes as a ratio of the number of convictions, 1990-2000

Source: United Nations Office on Drugs and Crime.

Caribbean, with one conviction being recorded for approximately every 15 recorded cases. Given the remarkably high levels of robbery in some Latin American countries (for example, Argentina and Ecuador) the attrition rate in respect of convictions reflected in figure VII gives cause for concern. Both North America and the European Union show one conviction for every nine cases of reported cases of robbery, just above the global average.

The data suggest that among all the countries that have reported data to the United Nations Survey of Crime Trends, and for the period 1980-2000, a conviction was likely to be achieved in one out of every four cases of homicide and one out of every eight cases of robbery. There are, however, considerable regional differences in such rates and the global averages reflect the fact that much of the survey data is received from developed countries. The true global average for obtaining convictions is, in all likelihood, much lower.

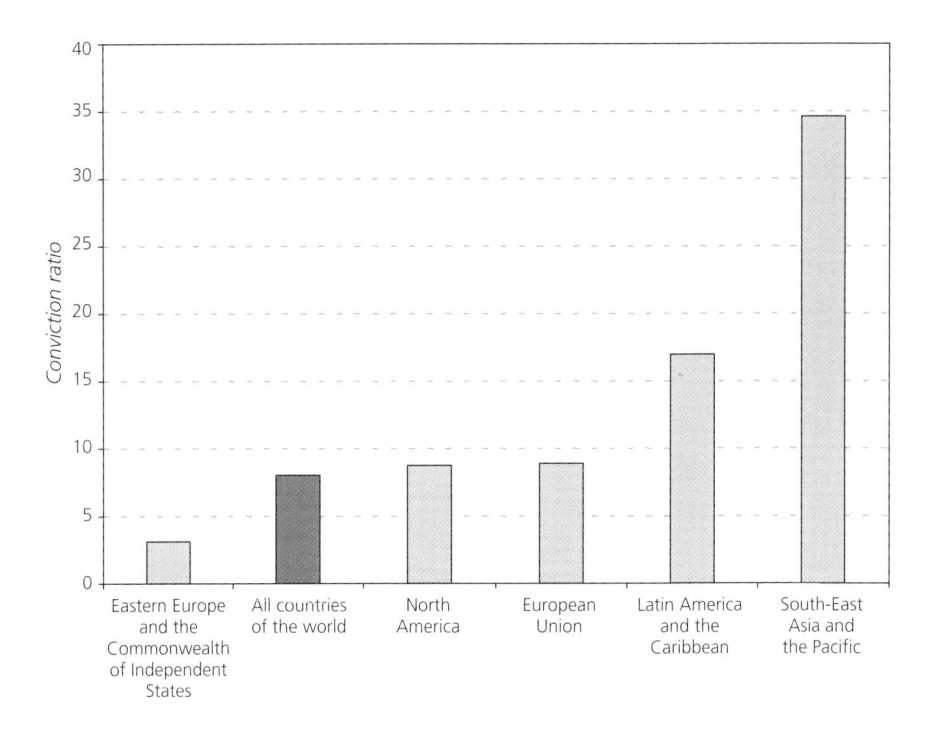

Figure VII. Comparative regional attrition rates for robbery: the number of recorded crimes as a ratio of the number of convictions, 1990-2000

[Bar chart showing conviction ratio by region:
- Eastern Europe and the Commonwealth of Independent States: ~3
- All countries of the world: ~8
- North America: ~9
- European Union: ~9
- Latin America and the Caribbean: ~17
- South-East Asia and the Pacific: ~35]

Source: United Nations Office on Drugs and Crime.

It should be noted in this context that in jurisdictions where reporting a case is unlikely to result in a prosecution or conviction (those countries with high attrition rates) the incentive for citizens to report crime is reduced.

If more comprehensive data sets on prosecutions and convictions are obtained over time, the United Nations surveys of crime trends have the potential to reflect much more clearly the comparative success rates of various criminal justice systems. Already, it should be noted, the data for the Seventh Survey (from which the three country comparisons above were drawn) are much more comprehensive than those of previous surveys. This is partly because the survey question has been refined, but also because the responding countries appear to provide better data, presumably due to advances in technology and more effective recording systems. Over time, therefore, the United Nations surveys of crime trends are likely to provide much more usable data in this regard.

Personnel and resources

A comparative measure of the number of inhabitants per police officer across the regions of the world is shown in figure VIII. The regional breakdown is the standard one used by the Statistics Division of the United Nations Secretariat. On average, there are just over 400 inhabitants for every police officer across the globe. Africa shows the highest number of citizens per police officer across all its regions, with East Africa in particular showing almost 1,000 inhabitants per police officer. Various subregions in Asia also appear to have comparatively small numbers of police officers per head of population. European, North American and Latin American jurisdictions all record higher numbers of police officers, with the Caribbean, in particular, displaying comparatively the smallest number of inhabitants per police officer.

Figure IX shows per capita figures for judges and magistrates for regions across the world. On average, there are 15,000 inhabitants for every judge or magistrate across the globe. Again, the results for Africa and parts of Asia indicate that there are comparatively few magistrates and judges per head of population. While Latin America and the Caribbean and South America have comparatively large numbers of police officers, they have comparatively fewer judges and magistrates. All regions of Europe (including Eastern Europe) and North America have comparatively large numbers of judges and magistrates.

The summary of the numbers of criminal justice personnel make it clear that simple numbers of criminal justice personnel (for example, police in Latin America or judges or magistrates in Eastern Europe) do not necessarily mean that levels of crime are lower. To explore the issue more fully, some attempt was made to compare expenditure on criminal justice across countries.

The United Nations Survey of Crime Trends requested States to provide budget figures for the various entities (police, prosecution services, courts and prisons) of the criminal justice system. Three factors complicated the analysis of those data. First, most countries only provided data on their police budget. Second, the Survey requested data only in the local currency. Finally, comparisons of spending on criminal justice across the world are of limited usefulness if they take into account only the absolute amounts of resources that were allocated. Thus, as in the case of international measures of defence expenditure, a measure is provided of the expenditure on policing as a percentage of gross domestic product (GDP). The budgets of all countries were converted to United States dollars for the purpose of the analysis. The results are shown in figure X.

Figure VIII. Number of inhabitants per police officer, by region or subregion, 1998-2000

Source: United Nations Office on Drugs and Crime.

On average, countries across the globe spend just under one per cent of their GDP on policing, with some countries spending significantly more than that.

The available evidence, although this is limited by the fact that data on developing countries are not always accessible or reliable, suggests that broad generalizations to the effect that developing countries spend far less on policing than do developed countries cannot be made. While some developing countries appear to spend comparatively little on policing (for example, Madagascar and Zambia), others spend considerably more.

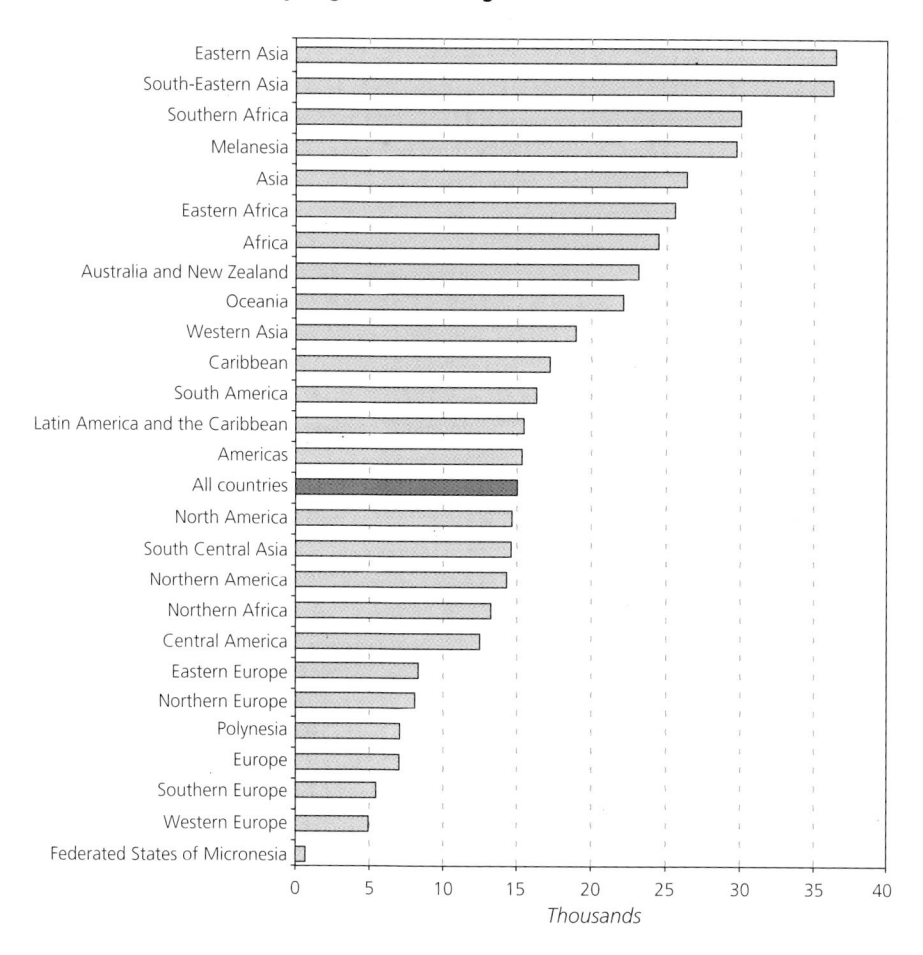

Figure IX. Number of inhabitants per judge or magistrate, by region or subregion, 1998-2000

Source: United Nations Office on Drugs and Crime.

Indeed, the majority of European countries appear to spend less than the global average on policing as a percentage of GDP.

A more detailed assessment of the link between crime levels and the personnel and expenditure devoted to criminal justice is beyond the scope of the present article. However, two tentative conclusions in that regard can be drawn. The first is that levels of personnel and expenditure patterns should be measured against levels of serious crime. When the number of personnel or expenditure on criminal justice is compared with levels of serious crime, it can be shown that countries with high levels of crime do, in fact, spend comparatively more on criminal justice, but often still relatively little

Figure X. **Expenditure on policing as a percentage of gross domestic product in selected countries and territories, 1988-2000**

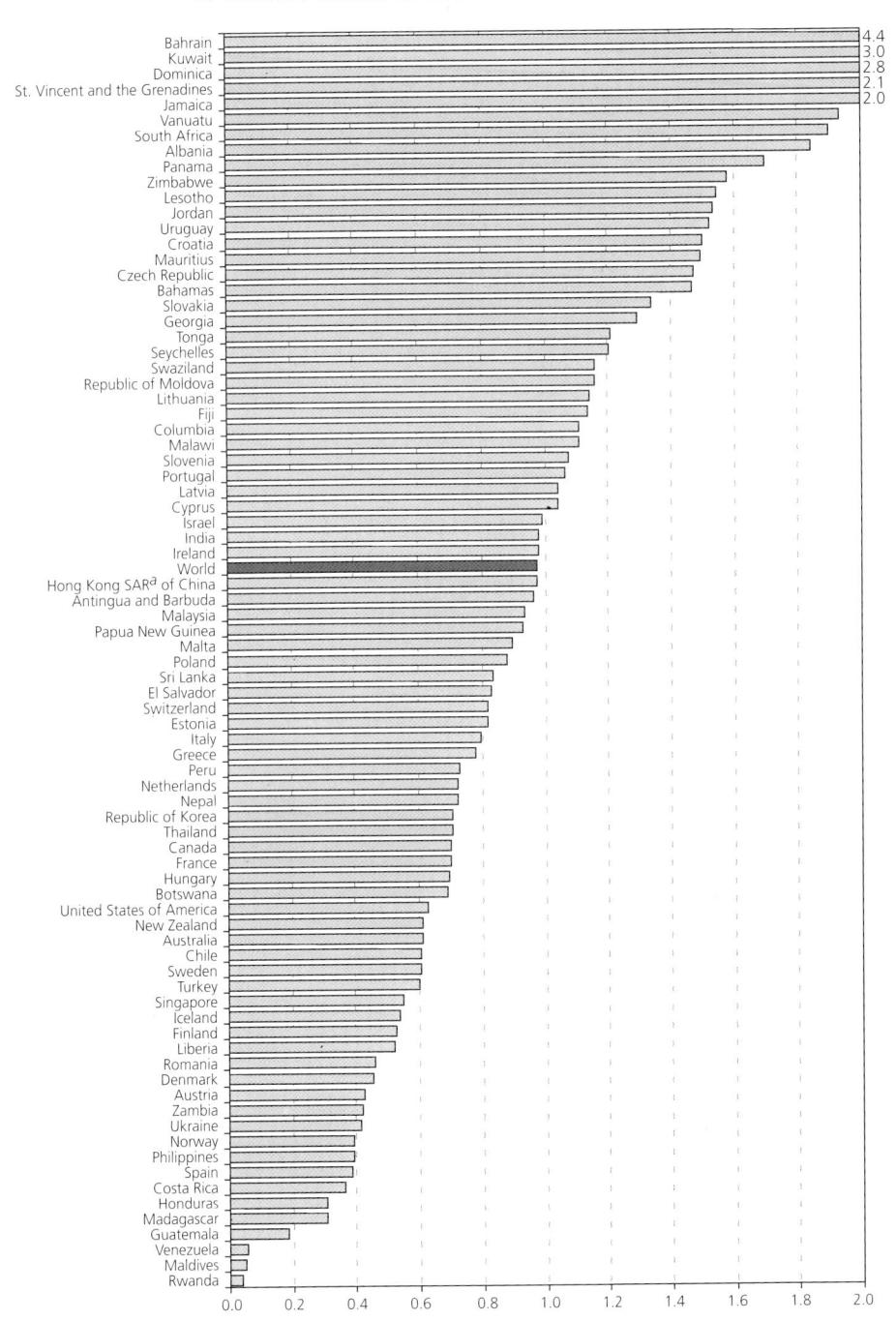

Country	Value
Bahrain	4.4
Kuwait	3.0
Dominica	2.8
St. Vincent and the Grenadines	2.1
Jamaica	2.0

Source: United Nations Office on Drugs and Crime.

[a] SAR = Special Administrative Region.

compared with recorded crime. Thus, to provide just one example, when the number of homicides per police officer is calculated, those countries with high levels of homicide, such as Colombia and South Africa, although spending above average, still feature particularly badly in a cross-country comparison of the number of homicides for every 1,000 police officers. When, for example, the number of homicides for every 1,000 police officers is calculated, the global average is 35, whereas the comparative figures for Colombia and South Africa are in the region of 200. For these reasons, the fact that comparative expenditure on criminal justice does not provide a measure of crime control capacity is widely acknowledged [14].

The second is that the distribution of expenditure between the police, prosecution services and courts must be seen as a key factor in understanding comparative expenditure levels on criminal justice. One possible explanation is that while developed countries appear to spend comparatively less on policing, their expenditure on other areas of the criminal justice system is simply much higher. An analysis of comparative expenditures on the various components of the criminal justice system, police, prosecution services and courts, was conducted. On average, among the countries reporting to the United Nations Survey of Crime Trends, just over half of all expenditure (56 per cent) was on the police, while the cost of the courts (29 per cent) and the prosecution services (15 per cent) made up the remainder (see figure XI).*

Figure XI. Breakdown of average expenditure on the police, prosecution services and courts

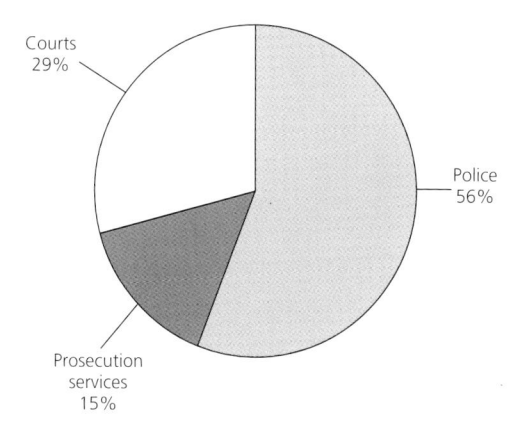

Courts 29%
Police 56%
Prosecution services 15%

Source: United Nations Office on Drugs and Crime.

---

*Data on expenditure on prisons has not been included, as that variable was not included in the latest sweep of the survey.

There are, however, significant differences across the world in the distribution of expenditure rates across components of criminal justice systems (see figure XII). The most pronounced in this regard is the data provided by various countries in Southern Africa, which show that expenditure patterns for the police take up a significant portion of the budget (84 per cent). By contrast, in North America, the overall expenditure breakdown between the police, courts and prosecution services is more balanced, 57 per cent being spent on the police, 32 per cent on the courts and 11 per cent on the prosecution services. While a more detailed analysis would be required to reach definite conclusions, it seems that developing countries (particularly those with an authoritarian past) spend comparatively much more on policing and much less on the courts and prosecution services. This finding may help to explain the relatively low proportions of police-recorded serious crimes leading to convictions in many developing countries.

Figure XII. Regional breakdown of expenditure on the police, prosecution services and courts: North America and Southern Africa

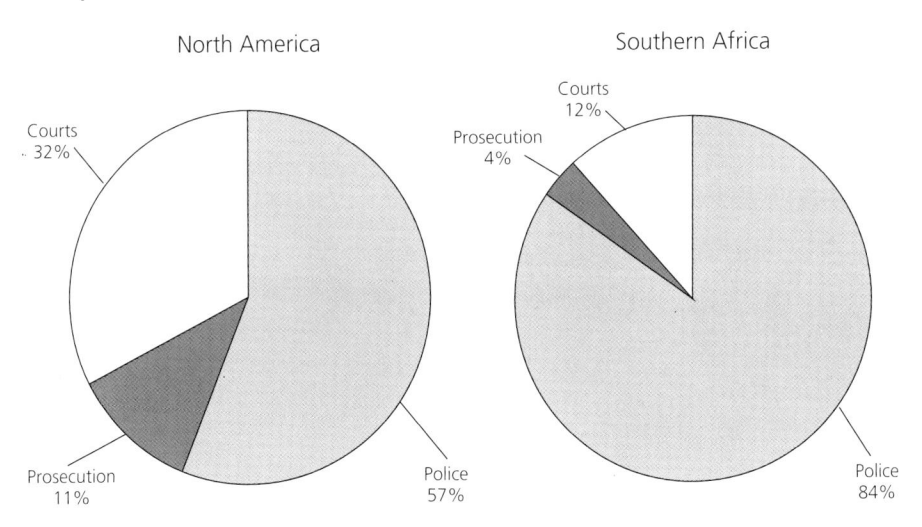

North America
- Courts 32%
- Prosecution 11%
- Police 57%

Southern Africa
- Courts 12%
- Prosecution 4%
- Police 84%

Source: United Nations Office on Drugs and Crime.

Conclusion

By selecting a range of data sets from the United Nations Survey of Crime Trends, the present article has sought to illustrate some recent crime trends and suggest possible ways in which the data can be used to assess the performance of criminal justice systems. The various drawbacks of the data have been highlighted, as have some possibilities for more effective application of the data. It should be emphasized that the data from the United Nations Survey of Crime Trends provides, despite the problems of reporting and recording, a relatively comprehensive reflection of crime trends in the developed world. Almost all developed countries have participated in the United Nations Survey of Crime Trends, many since its establishment in the 1970s, and so some important overall trends can be established.

An important and, by now, well-known (although little-understood) trend is the decline in overall crime rates in North America. While this has not been reflected as clearly in Western Europe, overall crime rates for the European Union countries can be regarded as having remained stable since the mid-1980s.

While data on middle-income, transitional and developing countries are less reliable, some important conclusions can also be reached. It is almost certainly the case that the proportion of crimes of violence are much higher than in developed countries and it is clear that countries in Latin America and sub-Saharan Africa suffer from comparatively high levels of homicide. In addition, the level of violent robbery in certain countries with economies in transition must be viewed with concern.

The data on less-developed countries in the United Nations surveys of crime trends are not well developed. This is, of course, a reflection not so much of the inadequacies of the surveys, but of the fact that in less-developed countries police-recorded crime data reflect a relatively small part of actual crime. It is clear that, in this regard, comparative measures of criminality can only be based on surveys of victimization in those countries. The successful completion in 2004 of the International Crime Victim Survey among developing countries is thus clearly a requirement for a fuller understanding of overall crime levels in the less-developed world. In addition, since many developing countries collect no substantial data on reported crime, capacity-building in relation to the collection, recording and publication of crime statistics would be a useful intervention in this regard.*

The present article has also provided some illustrations as to how the data from the United Nations surveys of crime trends can be used to measure criminal justice performance. While these are far from perfect and are based

---

*The United Nations *Manual for the Development of a System of Criminal Justice Statistics* (available at http://unstats.un.org/unsd/pubs/gesgrid.asp?id=293) provides a detailed review of the requirements for the effective collection, recording and publication of crime statistics.

on the assumption that better data can be collected over time, the United Nations surveys of crime trends will be able to provide an indication of the comparative effectiveness of various systems of criminal justice. In addition, such measures of efficiency and effectiveness can be compared with expenditure levels illustrated, for example, by the proportion of GDP that countries spend on criminal justice. There are indications of under-investment in prosecution services and courts in some developing countries, resulting in conviction rates that are too low and continuing high rates of serious crime. Such findings call for more systematic and precise analysis. There is no reason why, in the long run, more consistent measures cannot be developed, as they have been for health, education or military expenditure.

The implications of review for the future of the United Nations Survey of Crime Trends are the following: first, the overall number of countries reporting crime and criminal justice data to the United Nations Survey of Crime Trends should be increased, as well as the overall quantity of data reported by individual countries. A comparison of the Interpol data and those collected by the United Nations surveys of crime trends suggests that, despite the size of the current database, there is still substantial crime and criminal justice data that can be added. While many countries may not have reported crime data, even in the less-developed world criminal justice systems generally maintain a rudimentary set of statistics on their own performance.

Second, the reader may have noted that the last available data from the United Nations Survey of Crime Trends were for 2000, given that the various sweeps of the Survey have collected data for periods of between three and five years. If the United Nations Survey of Crime Trends is to be a relevant tool for international policy makers, there is little doubt that more up-to-date statistics must be collected in order to illustrate more recent trends. It should be possible, for example, to conduct the Survey every year or, perhaps more realistically, every two years.

Finally, while the United Nations Survey of Crime Trends provides a wealth of data, there have been few attempts to report regularly on its contents to those who make contributions to it. If data are collected more regularly, then the contents of the surveys of crime trends should also be published more regularly. If it was published more often, more information would be available to international policy makers in the area of criminal justice and fresh debates on global crime trends and the comparative effectiveness of criminal justice systems would be sparked.

References

1. Gordon Barclay and Cynthia Tavares, *International Comparisons of Criminal Justice Statistics 2000* (United Kingdom of Great Britain and Northern Ireland Home Office, 12 July 2002), No. 05/02. Available at www.homeoffice.gov.uk/rds/pdfs2/hosb502.pdf.

2. Pablo Fajnzylber, Daniel Lederman and Norman Loayza, "Inequality and violent crime", *Journal of Law and Economics*, vol. 45, No. 1 (2002).

3. United Nations, Office on Drugs and Crime, *Global Report on Crime and Justice*, Graeme Newman, ed. (New York, Oxford University Press, 1999).

4. Anna Alvazzi del Frate, "The voice of victims of crime: estimating the true level of conventional crime", *Forum on Crime and Society*, vol. 3, Nos. 1-2 (2003).

5. *Global Report on Crime and Justice . . .*, pp. 43-44.

6. Mark Shaw, *Crime and Policing in Post-Apartheid South Africa* (London, Hurst and Company, 2002).

7. Jan van Dijk, "Does crime pay? On the relationships between crime, rule of law and economic growth", *Forum on Crime and Society*, vol. 1, No. 1 (February 2001) (United Nations publication).

8. Ineke Haen Marshall, "Operation of the criminal justice system", *Crime and Criminal Justice in Europe and North America, 1990-1994*, Kristiina Kangaspunta, Matti Joutsen and Natalia Ollus, eds. (Helsinki European Institute for Crime Prevention and Control, affiliated with the United Nations, 1998).

9. John van Kesteren, Pat Mayhew and Paul Nieuwbeerta, *Criminal Victimisation in Seventeen Industrialised Countries: Key Findings from the 2000 International Crime Victims Survey* (The Hague, Netherlands, Ministry of Justice, 2000).

10. World Health Organization, *World Report on Violence and Health* (Geneva, 2002), pp. 9-11. Available at www.who.int/violence_injury_prevention/violence/world_report/wrvh 1/en/.

11. Mark Shaw, "Crime, police and public in transitional societies", *Transformation*, No. 49, 2002.

12. Rachel Neild, "Democratic police reforms in war-torn states", *Journal of Conflict, Security and Development*, vol. 1, No. 1 (2001).

13. Mark Shaw, *Democracy's Disorder? Crime, Policing and Citizen Responses in Transitional Societies* (Johannesburg, South African Institute of International Affairs, 2002).

14. Edgardo Buscaglia and Jan van Dijk, *Forum on Crime and Society*, vol. 3, Nos. 1-2 (2003).

GLOBAL INCARCERATION AND PRISON TRENDS

by Roy Walmsley*

Abstract

The present article provides an overview of the extent and ongoing trends in respect of global imprisonment and suggests that there is an urgent need to tackle a crisis that, while aimed at punishing individuals, may also prevent them from returning as effective and functioning members of society.

INTRODUCTION

The latest figures available indicate that more than 8.75 million people are being held in penal institutions around the world, either as pre-trial detainees (remand prisoners) or having been convicted and sentenced.** Since, according to the United Nations Population Fund report *The State of World Population, 2002,* there were about 6.2 billion people in the world in 2002, this means that the world prison population rate is approximately 140 per 100,000 citizens. To put it another way, about 1 out of every 700 persons in the world is being held in a penal institution. The countries with the highest prison populations are shown in table 1.

Figures in table 1, however, may be more a reflection of the size of the national population of each of the countries than of their practice in terms of incarceration. It is the prison population rate (per 100,000 of the national population) that must be used for a comparison of the numbers of people that countries are holding in their penal institutions. This is illustrated in figure I below, which shows the 24 countries and territories with the highest prison population rates in the world.

---

*Consultant, United Nations Office on Drugs and Crime; Consultant, European Institute for Crime Prevention and Control, affiliated with the United Nations; Associate, International Centre for Prison Studies, University of London.

**World Prison Population List. The List was first published in 1999 by the Research, Development and Statistics Directorate of the Home Office of the United Kingdom of Great Britain and Northern Ireland as *Research Findings No. 88* by Roy Walmsley. The fourth edition was published in 2003 [1]. The World Prison Brief, a comprehensive database of information on the prison systems of the world developed out of the List and is available on the Internet (www.prisonstudies.org). It is produced at the International Centre for Prison Studies, King's College, University of London. Important sources for these products include the United Nations surveys on crime trends and operations of criminal justice systems.

Table 1. Countries with the largest number of people held in penal institutions

Country	Prison population	Date
United States of America	1 962 220	31 December 2001
China	1 428 126[a]	mid-2001
Russian Federation	919 330	1 September 2002
India	281 380	1999
Brazil	233 859	December 2001
Thailand	217 697	mid-2001
Ukraine	198 885	1 September 2001
South Africa	176 893	14 June 2002
Islamic Republic of Iran	163 526	April 2002
Mexico	154 765	30 June 2000

[a]Sentenced prisoners only.

Figure I. Countries and territories with the highest prison population rates

Prisoners (per 100,000 inhabitants)

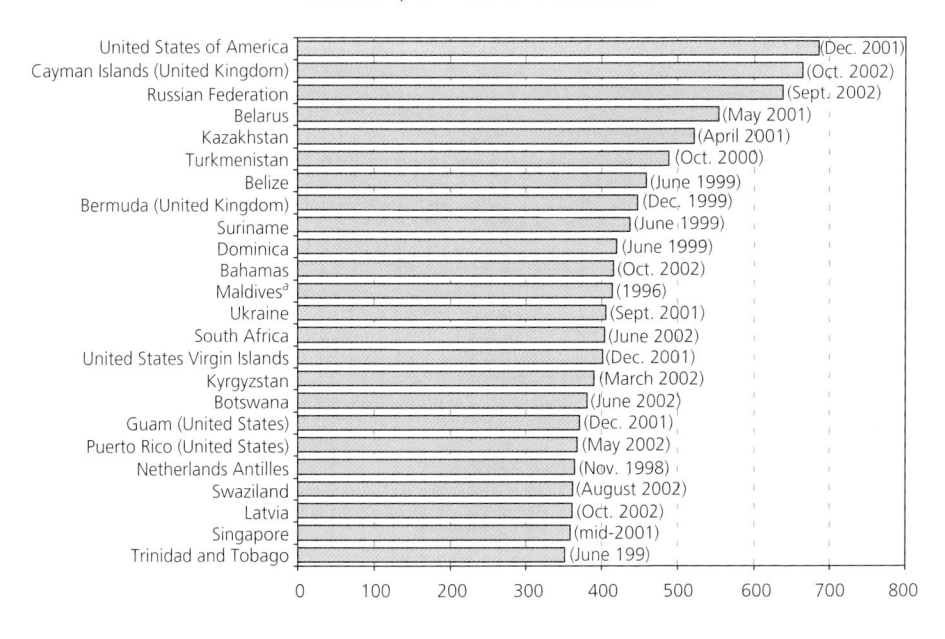

Country	Date
United States of America	(Dec. 2001)
Cayman Islands (United Kingdom)	(Oct. 2002)
Russian Federation	(Sept. 2002)
Belarus	(May 2001)
Kazakhstan	(April 2001)
Turkmenistan	(Oct. 2000)
Belize	(June 1999)
Bermuda (United Kingdom)	(Dec. 1999)
Suriname	(June 1999)
Dominica	(June 1999)
Bahamas	(Oct. 2002)
Maldives[a]	(1996)
Ukraine	(Sept. 2001)
South Africa	(June 2002)
United States Virgin Islands	(Dec. 2001)
Kyrgyzstan	(March 2002)
Botswana	(June 2002)
Guam (United States)	(Dec. 2001)
Puerto Rico (United States)	(May 2002)
Netherlands Antilles	(Nov. 1998)
Swaziland	(August 2002)
Latvia	(Oct. 2002)
Singapore	(mid-2001)
Trinidad and Tobago	(June 199)

[a]Sentenced prisoners only.

The United States of America has the highest prison population rate in the world: 686 per 100,000 of the national population at the end of 2001, almost five times the overall world rate. Second on the world list is the Cayman Islands, with a rate of 664 per 100,000 in October 2002. The Cayman Islands is a small Caribbean territory whose prison population is substantially inflated by the presence of drug smugglers who are nationals of other countries. After the United States and the Cayman Islands come the Russian Federation, Belarus, Kazakhstan and Turkmenistan (all former republics of the Union of Soviet Socialist Republics) and then Belize, Bermuda, Suriname and Dominica (all bordering on or islands of the Caribbean); these 10 countries and territories all have rates exceeding 400 per 100,000.

It is important to note that the countries and territories with the highest rates as illustrated in figure I do not necessarily have the most punitive criminal justice systems. They may simply have more serious crime to contend with or they may be more effective in solving and bringing to justice those who have committed a serious crime on their territory.

The countries and territories listed in figure I all have rates exceeding 350 per 100,000 inhabitants but it needs to be emphasized that this level of incarceration is much greater than is to be found in most parts of the world, since more than three fifths of countries (62.5 per cent) have rates below 150 per 100,000. Some of the lowest rates are to be found in smaller countries, although India, Indonesia and Nigeria are notable exceptions to this, and four countries in Western and Central Africa also have very low rates, despite national populations of over 8 million. One or two very small countries have artificially low rates, since they have only one, relatively insecure, prison institution and consequently have an arrangement with a neighbouring country, or in the case of a dependent territory with the administering Power, to hold prisoners who need more secure conditions or a more developed prison regime.

The countries and territories with the lowest prison population rates are shown in table 2 below.

Another important aspect of the situation relating to the world prison population is the fact that prison population rates vary considerably between different regions of the world and between different subregions of the same region. For example, in Africa the median rate for Southern African countries is more than seven times that for Central and West Africa. In the Americas, the median rate for the Caribbean countries is almost three times the rate for South American countries. In Asia, the median rate for the

Table 2. Countries and territories with the lowest prison population rates

Country or area	Prisoners per 100,000 inhabitants	Date
Faroe Islands (Denmark)	21	2000
Burkina Faso	24	September 2002
Nepal	25	1999
Vanuatu	25	mid-1999
Yugoslavia: Kosovo (Serbia and Montenegro)	27	May 2001
India	28	1999
Indonesia	29	mid-2001
Comoros	30[a]	1998
Solomon Islands	31	mid-1999
Gambia	34	September 2002
Nigeria	34	March 2002
Federated States of Micronesia	34	1997
Mali	35	February 2002
Angola	37	mid-2002
Guinea[b]	37	mid-2002

[a]Approximate figure.
[b]Conakry.

republics that were Central Asian countries of the former Union of Soviet Socialist Republics is almost eight times the rate for South Central Asian countries (mainly on the Indian subcontinent). In Europe, the median rate for Central and Eastern European countries is more than three times that for Southern European countries. The countries of Oceania (including Australia and New Zealand) have a median rate that is some 20 per cent below the world average.

These subregional variations are as follows:

Africa
Western and Central Africa 50
Eastern Africa 122
Northern Africa 124
Southern Africa 362

Americas
South America 107
North and Central America 164
Caribbean 297

Asia
South-Central Asia	54
West Asia	108
South-East Asia	118
East Asia	175
Central Asia	426

Europe
Southern Europe	69
Western Europe	85
Northern Europe	121
Europe/Asia	204
Central and Eastern Europe	213

Oceania 110

The data on subcontinents presented above are presented in figure II, beginning with the subregion with the highest prison population rate. It is clear that Central Asia, Southern Africa and the Caribbean have particularly large numbers of people behind bars.

Figure II. Prison population rates, by subregion

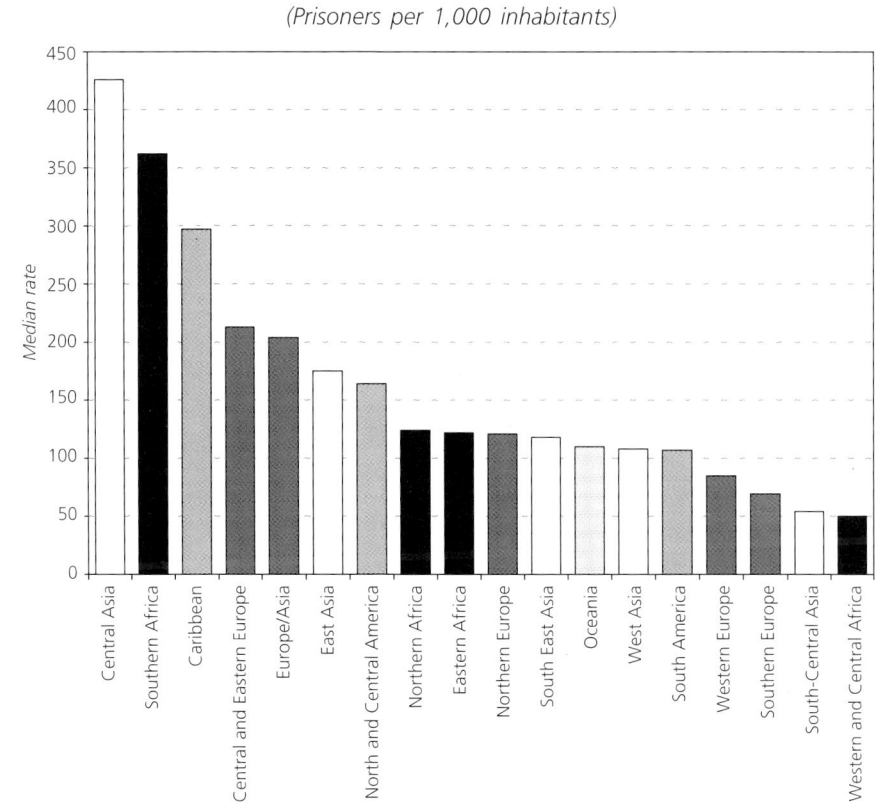

(Prisoners per 1,000 inhabitants)

Growth and trends in prison populations

Prison populations grew during the 1990s in many parts of the world. In Europe, they grew by over 20 per cent in almost all countries and by at least 40 per cent in one half of the countries; in the Netherlands, the prison population grew by 89 per cent. The prison population also grew in the six most populous countries in the Americas: the prison population growth was only 12 per cent in Canada, but between 60 and 85 per cent in Argentina, Brazil, Colombia, Mexico and the United States. Countries in other regions followed a similar growth pattern: 50 per cent in Australia, 38 per cent in New Zealand, 33 per cent in South Africa and 10 per cent in Japan. The general trend during the 1990s, at least in many developed countries, was for the prison population to increase, often by 40 per cent.

In recent years, it has been possible to monitor movements in the prison population of 173 countries. In 68 per cent of those countries, the prison population has risen. It has risen in 22 out of 36 African countries (61 per cent), in 28 out of 41 countries in the Americas (68 per cent), in 27 out of 31 Asian countries (87 per cent), in 32 out of 49 European countries (65 per cent) and in 8 out of 16 countries in Oceania (50 per cent), including Australia and New Zealand, the two largest countries in Oceania. There is thus a consistent pattern in all parts of the world. Some of the rises are substantial. For example, in Africa there have been rises of 38 per cent in Ghana over the last four years, 35 per cent in Malawi over four years, 24 per cent in South Africa over four and a half years and 26 per cent in Cameroon over five years.

In the Americas there have been rises of 50 per cent in El Salvador over three years, 50 per cent in Mexico over three and a half years, 38 per cent in the Dominican Republic over three and a half years and 40 per cent in Brazil over four years.

In Asia, there have been rises of 112 per cent in Cambodia over four years, 66 per cent in Thailand over three years and nine months, 51 per cent in Indonesia over four years and 35 per cent in Sri Lanka over four years.

In Europe, there have been rises of 45 per cent in Poland over two and a half years, 27 per cent in Finland over one year and eight months, 50 per cent in Greece over four years, 46 per cent in the former Yugoslav Republic of Macedonia over four years and 39 per cent in Ireland over four and a half years.

In Oceania, there has been a rise of 27 per cent in Australia over four years.

Although the trend is towards prison growth, there have been decreases in the prison population in almost one third of the countries where movements have been monitored. These, however, have generally been smaller than the increases in the other countries.

The most notable in Africa is a decrease of 22 per cent in Rwanda over three and a half years, mainly as a result of a reduction in the number of persons for suspicion of participating in the genocide of 1994. In the Americas, there has been a decrease of 28 per cent in Saint Vincent and the Grenadines over 3 years and nine months. In Europe, there have been decreases of 22 per cent in Switzerland over 2 and a half years, 31 per cent in Northern Ireland (United Kingdom) over four years and 21 per cent in Bulgaria over three years. No significant recent decreases have been monitored in the prison population of countries in Asia or Oceania.

Reasons for prison population growth

It is well established that crime rates alone cannot explain the movements in prison populations. In many countries, crime rates, including rates for the more serious crimes, have been stable or even decreasing, while prison populations have risen steadily. Part of this rise in prison populations is attributed by many experts to an increasing belief in a number of countries that prison is preferable to the alternatives.

As André Kuhn pointed out in 1997 [2], an increased fear of crime, a loss of confidence in the criminal justice system, disillusionment with positive treatment measures and the strength of retributionist philosophies of punishment all lie behind this belief. Loss of confidence in the system may lead to more draconian legislation being passed and harsher sentences may be used as emergency remedies to keep society integrated. Retributionist philosophies can readily be translated into popular demand for longer, tougher sentences. Such factors certainly appear to have led to a change in attitudes in some parts of Europe and North America among key groups (policy makers, members of the judiciary, prosecutors and the media) as well as among the general public.

Attitudes can also be influenced in the short term by isolated dramatic events, which can result in the public demanding a more punitive response to certain crimes and offenders. Such a demand may be accepted by both policy makers and the courts. After the media has moved on to other issues, the more punitive policy responses tend to remain in place.

A review of the factors that seem to have influenced the growth in the prison population in certain countries where major increases have recently occurred, indicates that the growth is the result of changes in policy. It is because of greater use of imprisonment, longer sentences and, in many European countries at least, more restricted use of parole or conditional release.

Why large prison populations matter

People often ask whether it matters if there is a large prison population. In principle, the more criminals that are locked up, the less crime they can commit; however, research has shown that, to have a significant effect on crime levels, far more people would have to be locked up and for longer periods—at great public expense—than even the countries that are most enthusiastic about imprisonment have been willing to do.

If a country finds it necessary to lock up a high proportion of its population, what does that say about the nature of the country? The countries with the highest prison population rates lock up more than 1 out of 80 of their male citizens, that proportion is much higher if boys too young to be imprisoned and older men are excluded (very few are included in prison populations). What does that say about the social cohesion of those countries? Does social cohesion matter? Should the emphasis be more on promoting social integration and less on locking people up?

Regardless of what a person might think about these broader issues, it is the practical considerations that are the most powerful in demonstrating that high prison population rates really do matter. High prison population rates and growth in prison populations invariably lead to overcrowding. The better-off countries manage to build more prisons as the numbers rise, but overcrowding still persists. Overcrowded prisons are a breach of United Nations and other international standards, which require that all prisoners are to be treated with respect to their inherent dignity and value as human beings, including being accorded a reasonable amount of space.

High prison population rates and growth in prison populations not only result in prison overcrowding, but also tend to be accompanied by a host of other major problems in prisons: restricted living space, poorer conditions of hygiene, poorer sanitation arrangements and less time for outdoor exercise. In many countries, there is insufficient bedding and clothing available for prisoners when there is significant prison population growth and the food is less satisfactory in terms of quality and quantity. Health care is also more difficult to administer effectively. There is more tension, more violence among prisoners and more violence directed against the staff. There is increased risk of self-injury and suicide.

When there is growth in prison numbers the ratio of staff to prisoners invariably falls. Reduced staff-to-prisoner ratios are likely to mean less effective supervision by the staff and less time for them to organize activities to ensure the existence of a positive regime that maximizes the chances of former prisoners being successfully reintegrated into the community. In particular, treatment programmes, including pre-release courses, are likely to be negatively affected. Furthermore, there are likely to be harmful effects on staff in terms of increased stress and sickness. There are also likely to be harmful effects on families and friends outside the prisons, because they rapidly become aware of the increased levels of tension and stress affecting prisoners and staff.

It has been said that prisons are "universities of crime" and imprisonment is "an expensive way of making bad people worse". It is clear that imprisonment in conditions of growth in numbers and overcrowding is even more damaging.

Measures for reducing high prison population rates

What can be done to reduce high prison population rates and to combat growth in prison populations? If it is accepted that imprisonment should be used as sparingly as possible, then even a prison population rate that is not among the highest may need to be reduced. Even when the overall prison population in a country is not particularly large, there will often be overcrowding, at least in some pre-trial prisons.

First of all, less use can be made of pre-trial (or remand) imprisonment. In many countries, suspects are detained in prison almost automatically once they are arrested. In other countries, it is known that pre-trial imprisonment is often unnecessary. Legislation needs to be in place to ensure that there are appropriate restrictions on the circumstances in which pre-trial imprisonment can be used, so that it is limited to cases where offences are particularly serious or where, for some other reason, it is clearly not in the public interest to allow the suspect to remain in the community.

Secondly, when a person is held in pre-trial imprisonment, the period should be as short as possible. In many countries, investigation procedures are long, and even when a decision has been taken to prosecute there are delays in arranging the court hearing because there is a backlog of cases. Legislation can be introduced to shorten the time allowed for investigation. Thirdly, it is important to increase the availability of alternatives to prison sentences. The existence of alternatives certainly does not guarantee that the prison population rate will not be high, but in many countries the courts have limited options: only fines, imprisonment and sometimes suspended imprisonment. Probation and community service have been introduced in a number of countries and are planned in others. Community service is showing signs of reducing prison population totals, for example in sub-Saharan Africa. Then there is the question of ensuring that there are actual reductions in the use of prison sentences for convicted offenders. In many countries, large numbers of persons are held in prison although they are not regarded by anyone as posing a danger to society or as having committed so serious a crime that only imprisonment could reflect its gravity. In other countries, such people are not imprisoned and prison population levels are lower. A wider application of the United Nations Standard Minimum Rules for Non-custodial Measures (the Tokyo Rules) (General Assembly resolution 45/110, annex) on alternatives to imprisonment is recommended.

Where prison sentences are unavoidable, they can be made as short as possible. Again there are vast disparities between the length of sentence that offenders are likely to get for a particular crime in one country and the length they would get in another. Although such disparities can be explained by differences in legislation and public opinion, it does not mean that longer sentences provide for more security of citizens. High prison population rates can be reduced by increasing the use of early release procedures, such as parole and conditional release. On the contrary, many countries have become more restrictive in granting early release. However, there are a number of advantages, from the point of view of the public and therefore from the point of view of potential victims to increasing the use of parole. The most obvious must be the assistance that parole can give to the reintegration of the offender into the community.

If the above-mentioned measures are ineffective in reducing the prison population, or cannot be applied, for example because they have not been legislated for or because they would not be acceptable in a particular country, then consideration can be given to the use of amnesty for less serious offenders who are approaching the end of their sentences. Amnesty is essentially a measure of short-term value, but if high prison population levels and overcrowding cannot be effectively combated in any other way, amnesty can play a useful role.

Finally, restorative justice is a measure that can be an alternative not only to the use of imprisonment, but also to the use of the criminal justice system itself. Restorative justice is increasingly being recognized as the way forward in a number of circumstances, not all of them involving minor offences. Although there is no concrete evidence that restorative justice has led to a reduction in prison populations, it is believed that it will play an increasing role in doing so as it is used more and more instead of criminal justice procedures, instead of imprisonment and during imprisonment, as a measure that is likely to create the conditions in which earlier release becomes possible.

Reducing high prison population rates: getting the measures accepted

It is one thing to identify the measures that can be taken to reduce high prison population rates and to combat prison population growth; it is another to persuade those concerned to take those measures. Merely changing laws and creating possibilities of new non-custodial sanctions are not enough. To get the measures accepted, it is necessary to convince all the key players in the criminal justice world. The policy makers, including government ministers, and legislators must be convinced; so must the judiciary and the police and prosecutors; and it is vitally important to convince the media and the general public. Policy makers and legislators must be helped to understand what imprisonment can achieve, what its limits are and what its dangers are. They must also fully understand the financial costs entailed in a high level of imprisonment. If they are not impressed by the arguments for greater humanity and social reintegration, they will sometimes be impressed by the expense of imprisoning so many people.

The judiciary obviously has a key role to play. Its members must also become fully aware of what imprisonment can and cannot achieve and of the harm it can do. All judges ought to be familiar with prison conditions and well informed about the opinions of prison experts, especially including those who work in prisons and with prisoners. They should also receive information concerning the impact of their sentences on prison population levels and, where possible, on the future criminal careers of those whom they sentence. Furthermore, they should be informed about sentencing disparities, although they may regard disparities between their own practice and that of others merely as a result of the difference in individual cases. Some judges are known to be resistant to anything that they view as a restriction on their discretion, and there is a possibility that information on disparities will lead as much to raising the level of more lenient sentences as to reducing the level of harsher ones. But the broader the picture they receive of practice in other jurisdictions, for example, and the better they are able to accept it through improved judicial training, the less of a risk this may be. Clearly, any policy of reducing the use of imprisonment and the length of sentences must win the hearts and minds of the judges.

The police and prosecuting authorities often exercise a major filtering influence in the criminal justice system and not only in respect of offenders whose crimes are so minor that they would be unlikely to receive sentences of imprisonment. Efforts to provide criminal justice officials with balanced information about imprisonment should extend to the police and prosecuting authorities. However, it is not just the criminal justice professionals that need to be persuaded. The media and the general public play a crucial role in many developed countries. The media are the source of a great deal of information, both true and false. It has been argued by Thomas Mathiesen [3] that, intentionally or not, the media have the effect of exerting pressure on policy makers to make decisions based less on principles than on what will be readily acceptable to the prejudices of the average voter, who is not well informed in such matters. Mathiesen suggests that this weakens the importance of national debate on fundamental issues of criminal policy. The media image is thus selective, simplified and skewed and drives discussion down to the level of the sound bite. If this analysis is accepted, it may well be that the public's fear of crime, and hostility towards offenders in general, needs to be counteracted by providing more accurate descriptions of offenders and the circumstances in which they commit their offences and by providing information on the functions of punishment, on the relative effectiveness of custodial and non-custodial measures and on the reality of prisons. The public is not generally aware of the problems faced in prisons, nor is it aware of the dangers of uncontrolled use of imprisonment or of its human and financial costs. Representatives of the media who are receptive to these issues can be drawn into a debate on how criminal justice should be reported. The basic requirement is for more responsible media coverage. Media watchdogs could be required to ensure that coverage of sensational and rare offences and incidents is balanced; at the very least such coverage should point out how rare such incidents are.

The International Crime Victim Survey includes a question on public attitudes towards punishment, asking the respondents what sentence they considered most appropriate for a recidivist burglar—a man aged 21 who is found guilty of burglary for the second time, having stolen a colour television. A community service order was seen as the most appropriate sentence in the industrialized countries providing results in the 2000 Survey: 41 per cent of respondents recommended it. Imprisonment was recommended by 34 per cent of respondents and was the first choice in half of the countries, the greatest support being in the United States, where 56 per cent of respondents opted for it. In Japan and the United Kingdom of Great Britain and Northern Ireland, over 50 per cent of respondents favoured imprisonment [4].

How successful can anyone hope to be in significantly influencing policy makers, judges, the media and the public in this way? Maybe many dramatic turnarounds cannot be expected, but every little bit helps and dramatic turnarounds are certainly not impossible. In Finland, for example, there was a steady downward trend in the prison population during the 1990s. The trend had started in the 1970s. Tapio Lappi-Seppala argues [5] that specific law reforms that were expressly designed to reduce the prison population were introduced, for example redefining laws and penalties concerning theft and increasing the use of suspended sentences and parole. Lappi-Seppala draws attention to the fact that the decisive factor was not the reforms themselves but the readiness of civil servants, the judiciary and the prison authorities to use all available means to bring down the number of prisoners. They had noticed that the neighbouring Scandinavian countries each had a much lower number of prisoners and that the figure for Finland was a legacy of Soviet influence on the country. That led a group of key individuals to recognize Finland's prison population rate as a problem and to produce a number of measures, not only law reforms and alterations to sentencing practice, but also low-level, day-to-day decisions, which all contributed to the desired result. According to the findings of the International Crime Victim Survey, public support for community service orders in Finland increased markedly after 1989, when the sanction was introduced in the country, suggesting that change in formal sentencing can increase support for alternatives to imprisonment. So, it can be done, if the determination can be created in the right quarters.

To do this, criminal justice experts need to ensure that the key people are well-informed; provide information to and stimulate discussion among opinion formers, the media and the general public; challenge media misrepresentations; draw attention to how similar countries or jurisdictions cope differently; and bring the key people together to promote policy discussions, leading to decisions as to the direction in which policy ought to move.

If steps are not taken to reduce high prison population rates and stem the growth, then the current 8.75 million in prison will soon become 10 million or more and a significant minority will be locked away, at great cost in human as well as financial resources, despite the fact that there is only a need to incarcerate a far smaller number, either to register abhorrence at what has been committed or to protect people from further serious crime.

References

1. Roy Walmsley, "World Prison Population List: fourth edition", *Findings*, No. 188 (London, Home Office Research, Development and Statistics Directorate, 2003).
2. André Kuhn, "Prison population: how many? why? what is to be done?", unpublished conference paper, 1997.
3. Thomas Mathiesen, "The media, public space and prison population", *Prison Population in Europe and North America: Problems and Solutions* (Helsinki, Ministry of Justice of Finland, 1997).
4. John van Kesteren, Pat Mayhew and Paul Nieuwbeerta, *Criminal Victimisation in Seventeen Industrialised Countries: Key Findings from the 2000 International Crime Victim Survey* (The Hague, Ministry of Justice of the Netherlands, 2000).
5. Tapio Lappi-Seppala, "The fall of the Finnish prison population", *Journal of Scandinavian Studies in Criminology and Crime Prevention*, vol. 1, No. 1 (2000), pp. 27-40.

PART TWO
Notes and action

MAPPING THE INHUMAN TRADE: PRELIMINARY FINDINGS OF THE DATABASE ON TRAFFICKING IN HUMAN BEINGS

by Kristiina Kangaspunta*

Abstract

Most of the traditional methods of collecting data cannot be applied to new forms of crime such as trafficking in human beings. The present article examines the qualitative information in the database of the Global Programme against Trafficking in Human Beings of the United Nations Office on Drugs and Crime. The database includes information about all aspects of such trafficking. The data collected are comparable between countries and regions and are divided into three main sections: country reports, characteristics of the victims of such trafficking and of the traffickers and trafficking routes. The article illustrates the complexity of the data entry process.

Analysis of the data confirms that trafficking in human beings is a gender-specific phenomenon, a sad manifestation of the rampant violence against women and girls. The results may be used as a basis for setting priorities for international cooperation and for gaining a deeper understanding of the profile of a given country.

INTRODUCTION

Trafficking in human beings has been one of the most heated topics in international criminological discourse for some years. Many issues have been debated, such as the definition of trafficking in human beings, the differences between such trafficking and smuggling of migrants, its connection with prostitution and the legal significance of the consent of victims, to mention just a few. On many of these issues experts hold widely varying opinions. However, the international community, government officials, intergovernmental and non-governmental organizations and researchers are all agreed on one thing: there is a dearth of reliable data on human trafficking.

A global database on trends in trafficking in human beings was established under the Global Programme against Trafficking in Human Beings of

---

*Crime Prevention and Criminal Justice Officer, Global Programme against Trafficking in Human Beings, United Nations Office on Drugs and Crime.

the United Nations Office on Drugs and Crime in order to systematically collect and collate open-source information on such trafficking. A broad range of sources is scrutinized for information on trends in such trafficking and the routes used, characteristics of victims and offenders and criminal justice responses. In the present article the preliminary results of the analysis of the database will be presented, focusing mainly on the qualitative information entered into the database. A global overview of the countries of origin, transit and destination, as well of the victims and offenders, will be provided.

What is trafficking in persons?

The first international document on trafficking in women was the International Agreement for the Suppression of the White Slave Traffic, which was adopted in 1904 and has been ratified by 12 States. In 1949 the Convention for the Suppression of the Traffic in Persons and of the Exploitation of the Prostitution of Others was adopted by the General Assembly (resolution 317 (IV), annex) and has subsequently been ratified by 49 States. However, these legal instruments do not provide a clear definition of trafficking in human beings.

In November 2000, the General Assembly adopted the Protocol to Prevent, Suppress and Punish Trafficking in Persons, Especially Women and Children, supplementing the United Nations Convention against Transnational Organized Crime (General Assembly resolution 55/25, annex II). For the first time, the international community has adopted an agreed definition of human trafficking. The Protocol against Trafficking in Persons aims at preventing and combating trafficking and strengthening international cooperation against trafficking.

The definition of the term "trafficking in persons" in the Protocol* includes three elements: *(a)* recruitment, transportation, transfer, harbouring or receipt of persons; *(b)* the use of improper means, such as force,

---

*Article 3, subparagraph *(a)*, of the Protocol reads: "'trafficking in persons' shall mean the recruitment, transportation, transfer, harbouring or receipt of persons, by means of threat or use of force or other forms of coercion, of abduction, of fraud, of deception, of the abuse of power or of a position of vulnerability or of the giving or receiving of payments or benefits to achieve the consent of a person having control over another person, for the purpose of exploitation. Exploitation shall include, at a minimum, the exploitation of the prostitution of others or other forms of sexual exploitation, forced labour or services, slavery or practices similar to slavery, servitude or the removal of organs."

abduction, fraud or deception; and *(c)* the objective of exploitation, such as sexual exploitation, forced labour, servitude or slavery. States that ratify the Protocol are obliged to enact domestic laws making those activities criminal offences, if such laws are not already in place. The Protocol also requires States to take steps to protect and support victims of trafficking, who should be entitled to confidentiality and protection against offenders. This should include general protection as well as specific forms of protection when a person is providing evidence or assistance to the police or is appearing as a witness for the prosecution. Social benefits, such as housing, medical care and legal or other counselling, are optional requirements.

The United Nations Convention against Transnational Organized Crime (General Assembly resolution 55/25, annex I) is also supplemented by the Protocol against the Smuggling of Migrants by Land, Sea and Air (resolution 55/25, annex III). The definition of "smuggling of migrants" in that Protocol includes procurement of illegal entry of a person into a country of which the person is not a national or a permanent resident in order to obtain direct or indirect financial or other material benefit.* It is important to note the difference between the definitions of "trafficking in persons" and "smuggling of migrants", even though in reality it is sometimes difficult to draw a line between the two. According to Kelly and Regan [1], Murray [2] and Salt [3], smuggling of migrants is usually limited to illegally transporting the person to the country of destination, after which the relationship between the smugglers and smuggled persons terminates. In trafficking, on the contrary, persons are delivered to organizations or individuals who have paid for their delivery and the trafficked persons must, after the delivery, repay their debt to the organizers through prostitution or forced labour.

Problems of data on trafficking in human beings: availability and reliability

There has been a boom in recent years in information on trafficking in persons, although the reliability of that information remains a problem. New reports, manuals, articles and books seem to be published every week. However, most of the information is reporting on individual cases or is

---

*Article 3, subparagraph *(a)*, of the Protocol reads: "'Smuggling of migrants', shall mean the procurement, in order to obtain, directly or indirectly, a financial or other material benefit, of the illegal entry of a person into a State Party of which the person is not a national or a permanent resident."

prepared for advocacy purposes. If figures on such trafficking are given, they are usually based on published estimates of the level of trafficking and in most cases there is no explanation of how those figures were calculated [4].

Reliability of data remains a problem with most of the data sources. Because of the difficulties in data collection, reliable data are difficult to find. Even though some high-quality research exists in the field of trafficking in human beings [1, 5-7], most of the data are based on "guesstimates", which, in many cases, are used for advocacy or fund-raising purposes.

The question of whether global estimates of the scale of trafficking in humans serve any serious policy purposes should be posed. For other serious crimes, such as homicide, assault or rape, global estimates are usually not given even though there are considerable problems with the data in some regions of the world [8]. The global estimates on the numbers of persons involved in trafficking are always vague and cannot serve as a reliable knowledge base for policy planning. Thus it remains questionable whether this type of information is needed at all. For this reason, in the present article, no global estimates on the scale of trafficking in humans will be given.

Global mapping, based on the identification of the main countries involved in trafficking in humans, might be useful for planning and evaluation purposes. Mapping "hot spots" can give valuable information on the nature and situation of such trafficking, such as origin, transit and destination countries, as well as involvement of organized criminal groups in different countries and the main routes used. That knowledge can be used when developing cooperation between practitioners in the field of prevention, victim assistance and criminal justice responses and monitoring the impact of those actions. In addition, carefully collected and analysed national and regional data might yield profiles useful for developing regional cooperation in the fight against trafficking in humans.

The database of the United Nations Office on Drugs and Crime has been designed to include information dealing with all relevant aspects of trafficking from open sources. The main sources include official reports from Governments, information disseminated by intergovernmental and non-governmental organizations, research reports, conference material and media reports. In order to assess the level of reliability of sources, the database includes a field for the confidence level for each one, on a scale of 1 to 5, the default value for confidence being in the middle. For each source, the minus and plus factors influencing the confidence level are reviewed. For example, factors reducing the confidence levels include the fact that the figure is based on an extrapolation of a small sample. Factors increasing confidence include, for example, figures on real cases dealt with by the police.

Comparability

Some existing data collection initiatives gather information either globally or regionally (see annex). Such initiatives usually collect both quantitative and qualitative information on legislation, victim assistance, trafficking routes and other related information. Because of the nature of the information, in most cases the data are not comparable. One of the main objectives of the Global Programme against Trafficking in Human Beings database is to collect data that can be compared between different countries and regions. There are well-known problems that are common to all efforts to gather comparative data on crime, such as imprecise definitions, inaccurate classifications and differences in units of count used. Even crimes that might be considered to be covered by more or less similar definitions such as homicide are difficult to compare between countries [9]. With new forms of crime such as trafficking in humans, most of the traditional methods of collecting data cannot be used. Major problems with a comparative analysis include some of the following drawbacks:

(a) The lack of specific legislation on trafficking in persons resulting in the absence of official criminal justice statistics on cases involving trafficking in humans, such as number of police-recorded cases and number of persons prosecuted and convicted. Where legislation on trafficking in persons is available, the legal definitions vary considerably from one country to the other. For example, the legislation may address only some forms of trafficking in persons: such as trafficking in women for sexual exploitation or trafficking in children. In such cases official statistics include only some types of trafficking crime;

(b) In some countries, there is no clear distinction in the official statistics between cases involving trafficking in humans and those involving smuggling of migrants. This is also usually based on the lack of clear legal definitions of the two crimes. In other countries, the crimes are clearly distinguished by the legislator but not in law enforcement practice: the police might prefer to investigate some of the human trafficking cases as migrant smuggling crimes because often collection of evidence is easier. As a general rule, migrant smuggling investigations lead to successful prosecutions more often, since the testimony of the trafficking victims, which is usually difficult to obtain because of the fear of retaliation by traffickers or deportation by authorities, is not needed. For that reason human trafficking cases are often entered as migrant smuggling cases in official criminal justice statistics;

(c) There are very few countries that provide official statistics on cases involving human trafficking. The *Bundeskriminalamt*, the German criminal police, has published a comprehensive yearly report on crimes involving such trafficking since 1999 [10]. The first report of the Dutch National Rapporteur on Trafficking in Human Beings [5] gives detailed information on the national situation and includes figures also on victims, investigations and prosecutions. A national rapporteur on trafficking in women also operates in Sweden, submitting yearly reports on the situation in that country since 1998 [11];

(d) It is generally understood that statistics on the number of police-recorded crimes, prosecutions and convictions do not reflect actual levels of crime but rather give information on the operations of criminal justice systems. When action by the relevant authorities is increased, more cases are registered in the crime statistics. For crimes such as assault, rape or robbery, victimization surveys give more reliable figures on the true level of crime. In such surveys, samples of people are asked about their victimization experiences over a certain period of time [12]. General victimization surveys cannot be used to collect data on the number of trafficking victims because the crime is not common enough to be represented in a small sample of the population. However, a focused victimization study on trafficking experiences could be carried out among, for example, young women from developing countries returning from abroad. Several analyses have been made of data collected by service-providing non-governmental organizations on their clients. However, such data are usually not collected with standardized instruments and their reliability is difficult to assess.

The International Organization for Migration has systematically entered information on trafficking victims assisted by it into a database, using a standardized methodology. It includes both qualitative and quantitative information on numbers of victims assisted, their country of origin, age, trafficking route and the method in which they were trafficked [13-14].

The Global Programme against Trafficking in Human Beings has, together with the United Nations Interregional Crime and Justice Research Institute, developed a questionnaire for the systematic collection of data on the experiences of victims. The study will be repeated in different countries, yielding comparative data on victims' experiences. Instruments have also been developed to collect data from criminal justice practitioners in different countries. A pilot test in the Philippines [7] revealed that the fact that cases involving migrant smuggling and trafficking were not clearly separated in the legislation had an impact on, for example, non-governmental organizations that provided services to victims. During the data collection phase it became obvious that most of the persons who had been assisted had been repatriated after their illegal immigration into a foreign country through a smuggling operation. However, they were introduced to the researchers as trafficking victims. Interviews with the criminal justice practitioners also suffered from the same problem. Practitioners questioned about trafficking in humans mainly provided information on cases that involved smuggling but not trafficking.

Collecting data for the database on trends in trafficking in human beings

The United Nations Office on Drugs and Crime database on trafficking trends has been designed to collect a wide range of open-source information on trafficking in human beings. The information may come in the form of official government statistics, reports of research institutes or of intergovernmental and non-governmental organizations, but may also be drawn from newspaper articles and news agency bulletins.

As with other, more traditional types of crime, more data are available in developed countries than in developing countries. This is also reflected in the collection of data for the database. To date, information from 284 sources has been entered, most of it originating in developed countries. Many of the sources include data from different parts of the world, especially those published by international organizations. However, the predominant use of data from Western sources is likely to have introduced a bias in the data set and more efforts must be made to collect information from other regions of the world.

The collected data were entered into three different sections of the database:

   (a) *Section 1. Country reports*. Estimates on the volume of human trafficking in a given country, including trafficking to, within, through and from the country; trafficking for sexual exploitation or forced labour; and persons encountered and ultimately cases dealt with by the criminal justice system;

   (b) *Section 2. Profiles*. Characteristics of victims of trafficking or the traffickers: nationality, sex and age distribution;

   (c) *Section 3. Trafficking routes*. Information on countries included in the routes used for trafficking in humans.

The information obtained under sections 1 and 2 is primarily of a numerical nature, even though some of the victim characteristics may also be entered in free-form text fields. This ensures, at least to some degree, that the level of detail is not compromised by the emphasis of the database on quantitative data. The information gathered in the section of the database on trafficking routes is mostly non-numeric. However, numerical information can also be entered in that section. For the purpose of analysis, the data can be combined with data on the volume of human trafficking in a country obtained from section 1.

The database has been designed so that it is possible to include as wide a range of source material as possible in the final analysis. The flexibility of the database to incorporate a variety of information complicates extracting data from the database, because the same type of information can potentially be entered into more than one section. For that reason, in the reporting phase, the data stored in different sections of the database can be combined. For example, the number of persons trafficked to a country can be retrieved both from the country report section and from the section on trafficking routes.

As mentioned earlier, the database collects both qualitative and quantitative information about human trafficking from a variety of different sources. Those sources usually provide several "cases" about which information can be entered into the database. The cases can include information about different numbers of individual victims, offenders or police responses. The following example illustrates the complexity of the process of data entry:

Case

In July 2002, the Guatemalan police liberated nine El Salvadoran girls who had been trafficked in the same year from El Salvador to Guatemala and sexually exploited in a Guatemalan brothel. The rescued children were between 14 and 17 years of age. Two Guatemalan men, aged 25 and 30, who had allegedly exploited the girls were arrested.

Information suitable for the sections on "country reports" and "profiles":

    (a) Trafficking to a country: Guatemala;

    (b) Trafficking from a country: El Salvador;

(c) Reference year: 2002;

(d) Purpose of trafficking: sexual exploitation;

(e) Victims' profile: nine girls, aged between 14 and 17 (children), nationals of El Salvador;

(f) Offender's profile: two males, aged between 25 and 30, nationals of Guatemala;

(g) Criminal justice response: nine victims encountered (by the authorities), two suspects encountered (in the database, this type of "case study information" is separated from more general information on criminal justice action and is not used for national estimates).

Information suitable for the section on "trafficking routes":

In general, the route can be given a name and a number of stages depending on the number of transit countries. If there are no transit countries indicated, the route consists of two stages, origin and destination. If one transit country is indicated, this is referred as a three-stage route.

In this case, the country involved in stage one, the country or origin, is El Salvador. Stage two, the destination, is Guatemala. As regards stage two, the following information can be inserted: the number of trafficked persons was nine, they were girls and they were trafficked into the country. There is also a check box to show that they were sexually exploited. Even though the information can be entered into two different sections, at the analysis level, it is referred to only once.

Source: Report of the Guatemalan Police, 2002.

In the analysis phase, different types of information can be retrieved for a comparative analysis. The following are some preliminary results based on the 284 sources (reports and so on), and 3,671 cases included in the database so far. The preliminary results, which are presented below, focus on qualitative information and estimates of the size of trafficking flows are not included. They will be analysed at a later stage, when the number of sources and cases has been increased. Criminal justice responses such as number of investigations, prosecutions and convictions are also not discussed because more systematic data collection in that field is required.

Countries of origin, transit and destination

To assess how much a country is affected by the trafficking phenomenon, the number of citations as country of origin, transit or destination can be counted. In total, 147 countries are mentioned, at least once, as a country of origin. Among the most frequently cited countries of origin, in descending order, are the Russian Federation, Ukraine and Nigeria. If data are examined by region, it can be seen that countries in Asia are most frequently cited as countries of origin, the member States of the Commonwealth of Independent States (CIS) and African countries being cited second and third, respectively (figure I). Central and Eastern European countries were cited less often as countries of origin. There was a relatively small number of citations in Latin America and only a few citations referring to developed countries.

Figure I. Number of times a country was cited as a country of origin, by region

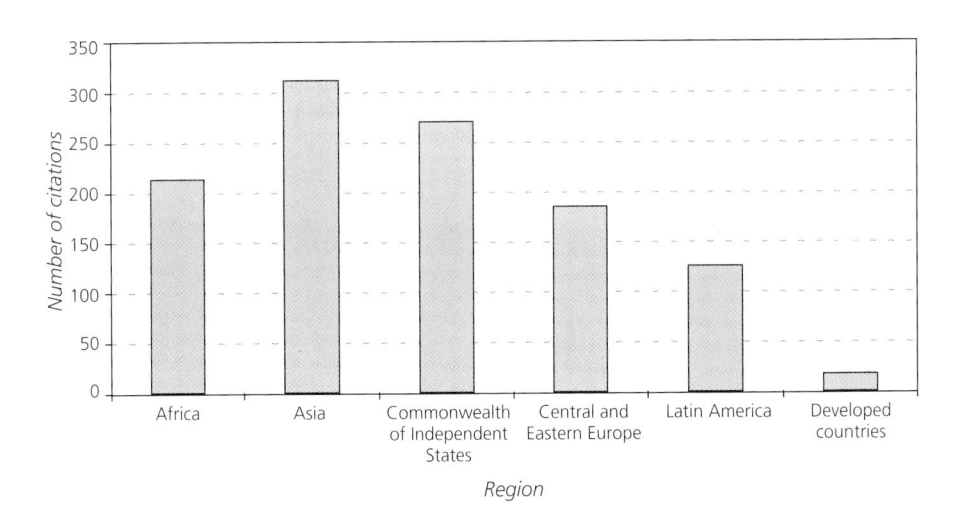

Citations referring to transit countries are much fewer than references to countries of origin. In total, 96 countries were mentioned as transit countries and the most frequently cited countries were in Central and Eastern Europe, as shown in figure II. The CIS member States and Latin American countries are less frequently cited as transit countries.

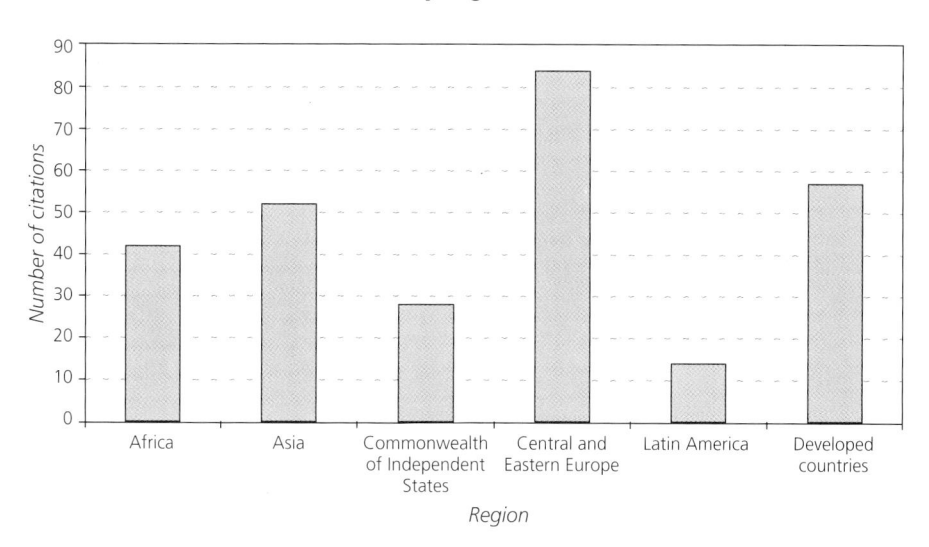

Figure II. Number of times a country was cited as a country of transit, by region

[Bar chart showing number of citations by region: Africa ~42, Asia ~52, Commonwealth of Independent States ~28, Central and Eastern Europe ~84, Latin America ~13, Developed countries ~57]

In total, 150 countries were cited as countries of destination by different sources (figure III). The most frequently mentioned destination countries included in descending order, the United States of America, several European Union countries and Japan. Regionally, the main destination countries were found in the developed world, Asia being the second most cited region. Central and Eastern Europe and Africa were also cited as destination regions. Citations referring to Latin American countries and CIS member States were relatively few.

When comparing the data globally, some regional characteristics can be found. Considering the global inequalities in affluence, it is not surprising that Africa, Asia and the CIS member States were the main regions where victims of trafficking were recruited. It should also not come as a surprise that developed countries found themselves at the end of the trafficking route. However, less obvious were the results concerning Central and Eastern Europe, indicating that this is the major transit region. Interesting also was the fact that Asia figured equally as a region of origin and of destination, as shown in figure IV.

In considering the Central and Eastern European countries as transit countries, it must be kept in mind that the number of sources mentioning them as transit countries was relatively low. A country has been indicated as a transit country only if this was explicitly stated in the source. A fictitious example might be information saying that children were trafficked from

Figure III. **Number of times a country was cited as a country of destination, by region**

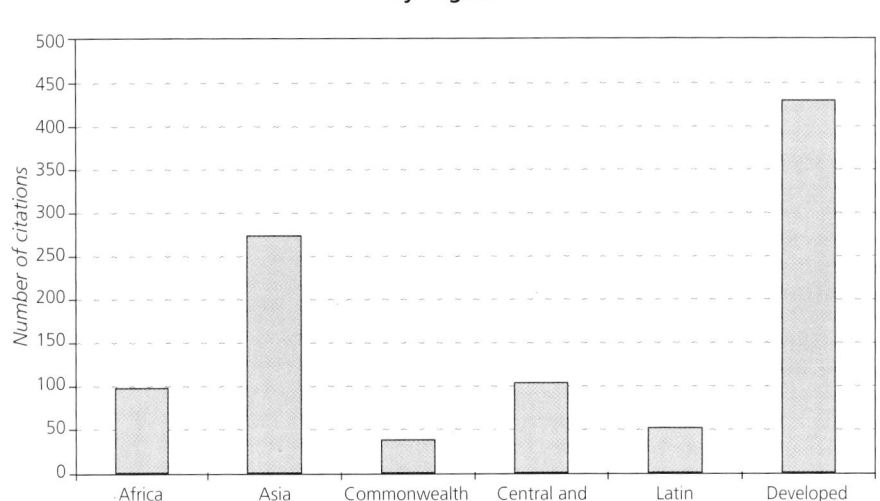

Figure IV. **Number of times a country was cited as a country of origin, transit or destination, by region (as a percentage of all citations)**

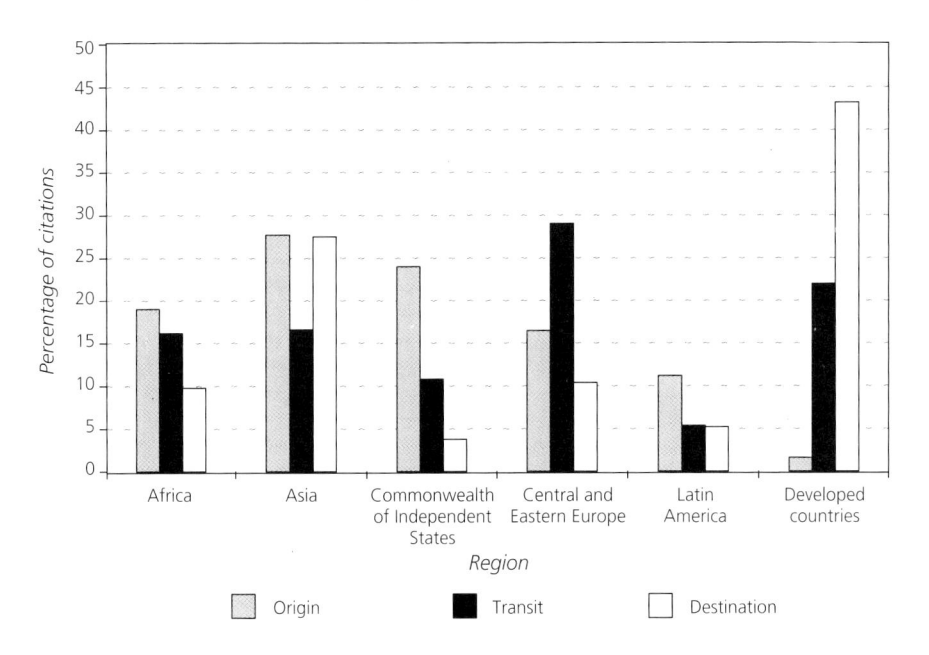

country A to countries B and C and then to country D. In this case, A is entered into the database as a country of origin, D as country of destination and B and C as countries of transit. Keeping this in mind, there is reason to believe that the Central and Eastern European region is indeed a major transit area. The first reason is, of course, its geographical position between north and south and east and west. In addition, the situation of countries of the region with economies in transition, where the control of the authorities might not be as strict as in Western Europe, may attract traffickers to look for safe routes. High levels of corruption among customs and police officers may also facilitate criminal activities. In many Western European countries, current visa regulations allow persons to stay in a country without any other authorization for up to three months, which facilitates final entry from Central and Eastern Europe into Western Europe.

The emerging picture of Asia as a region of both origin and destination is also worth examining in greater detail. It should be noted that Japan, as one of the top destination countries, was not included in the Asian region, but is included in the category of developed countries. If the region is again divided into subregions the picture becomes clearer, as presented in figure V.

The main countries of origin were found in South-East Asia and in South-Central Asia.* The main countries of destination were in West Asia and in South-East Asia.** South-East Asia was also the main transit area in the region, so the subregion seemed to combine all phases of the trafficking process. East Asia was mentioned slightly more as a receiving area than as a region of origin or transit.*** Each subregion thus showed a distinct profile in terms of the different stages of trafficking.

---

*Countries cited as countries of origin in South-East Asia were: Brunei Darussalam, Cambodia, Indonesia, Lao People's Democratic Republic, Malaysia, Myanmar, Philippines, Singapore, Thailand and Viet Nam; countries cited as countries of origin in South-Central Asia were: Afghanistan, Bangladesh, Bhutan, India, Islamic Republic of Iran, Nepal, Pakistan and Sri Lanka.

**Countries cited as countries of destination in West Asia were: Bahrain, Iraq, Kuwait, Lebanon, Oman, Qatar, Saudi Arabia, Syrian Arab Republic, Turkey, United Arab Emirates and Yemen; countries cited as countries of destination in South-East Asia were: Brunei Darussalam, Cambodia, Indonesia, Lao People's Democratic Republic, Malaysia, Myanmar, the Philippines, Singapore, Thailand and Viet Nam.

***Countries and territories cited as destinations in East Asia were: Hong Kong Special Administrative Region of China, Macao Special Administrative Region of China, Mongolia, Republic of Korea and Taiwan Province of China.

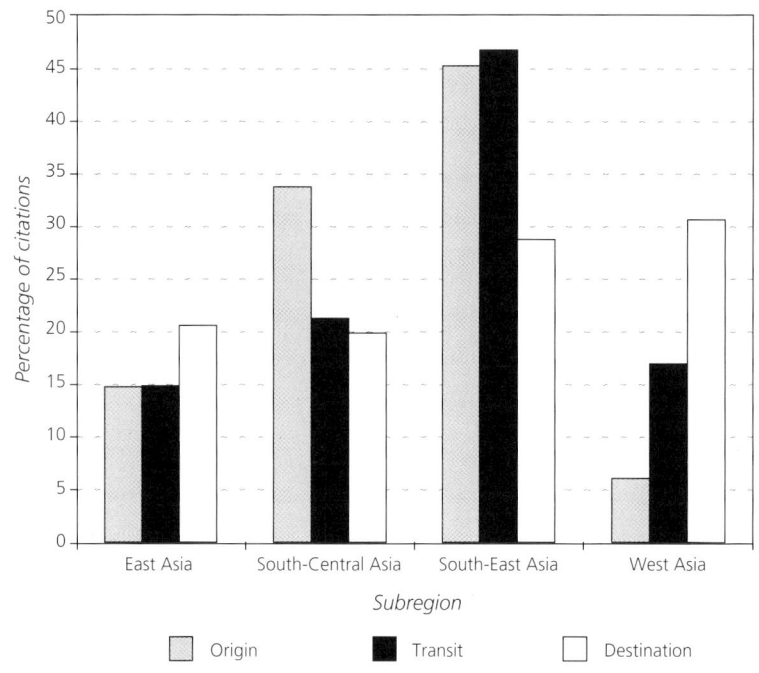

Figure V. Number of times a country was cited as a country of origin, transit or destination, Asia, by subregion[a] (percentage of all citations)

[a]The division is based on the composition of macrogeographical (continental) regions and component geographical regions used by the Statistical Division of the Secretariat (see www.un.org/Depts/unsd/methods/m49/m49regin.htm, accessed on 11 November 2003).

Profile of the victim

The data collected on victims concerns their nationality, sex and age, as well as the form of exploitation through which they are victimized. In total, 95 countries have been identified as home countries of victims of trafficking. The most frequently mentioned countries are, in descending order, Ukraine, the Russian Federation, Nigeria, Albania, Romania, the Republic of Moldova, Bulgaria, China, Thailand, the Czech Republic, Lithuania, Poland, Belarus and Latvia. As can be expected, the list of home countries closely paralleled that of countries already identified as countries of origin.

Where such information could be obtained, women were reported to be victims of trafficking in 83 per cent of the cases entered into the database. Men were reported to be victims in 4 per cent and children in 48 per cent of the cases. The total percentage does not add up to 100 because any one case could include combinations of women, men and children as victims. For example, a case could include information about a group comprising women and children trafficked from one country to another. Because the information was based on the number of cases in which women, men or children were mentioned as victims, the case in question would emerge twice, once in connection with women and again in connection with children.

Information was also collected on the type of exploitation suffered by the victims in the country of destination after their recruitment and transportation. It included information of two main types, namely, on sexual exploitation and on forced labour. The analysis was based on 3,671 cases. Of those cases for which the information was available, more than 80 per cent were for purposes of sexual exploitation and 19 per cent for forced labour.

If one examines women, men and children as separate groups of victims and how those groups were exploited at the end of the trafficking process, it can be seen from figure VI that, of all the cases in which sexual exploitation was reported, women were by far the largest group of victims, followed by children. Cases in which men were reported to be victims of sexual exploitation were rare. Cases of forced labour reported are presented in figure VII. Children constitute the largest group included in the cases of forced labour, followed by women. Again, men were seldom reported to be victims of forced labour. The latter may, however, also reflect a bias in the sources consulted.

If women, men and children are examined separately as victims of trafficking, the following results emerge (see figure VIII):

   (a) In 85 per cent of cases where women were reported to be the victims, they were said to be trafficked for sexual exploitation and in 2 per cent of the incidents for forced labour, while 13 per cent of cases included both types of exploitation;

   (b) Of cases where men were reported to be the victims, 16 per cent involved trafficking for sexual exploitation and 24 per cent for forced labour, with 60 per cent of cases including both types of exploitation;

   (c) As regards cases where children were reported to be the victims, in 70 per cent of the incidents children were said to be trafficked for sexual exploitation and in 13 per cent for forced labour and 18 per cent of cases included both types of exploitation.

When the focus was on the number of citations as country of destination for the purpose of sexual exploitation, the most cited country was Italy, followed by the United States and Germany. With forced labour the picture was somewhat different and the most cited countries were, in descending order, the United States, the United Arab Emirates, Gabon and Côte d'Ivoire.

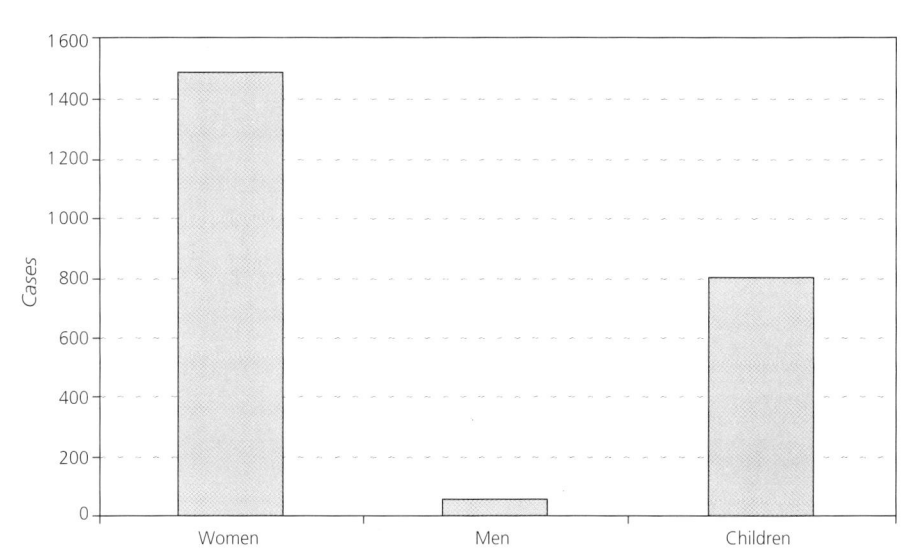

Figure VI. Number of cases of sexual exploitation of women, men and children

Figure VII. Number of cases of forced labour involving women, men and children

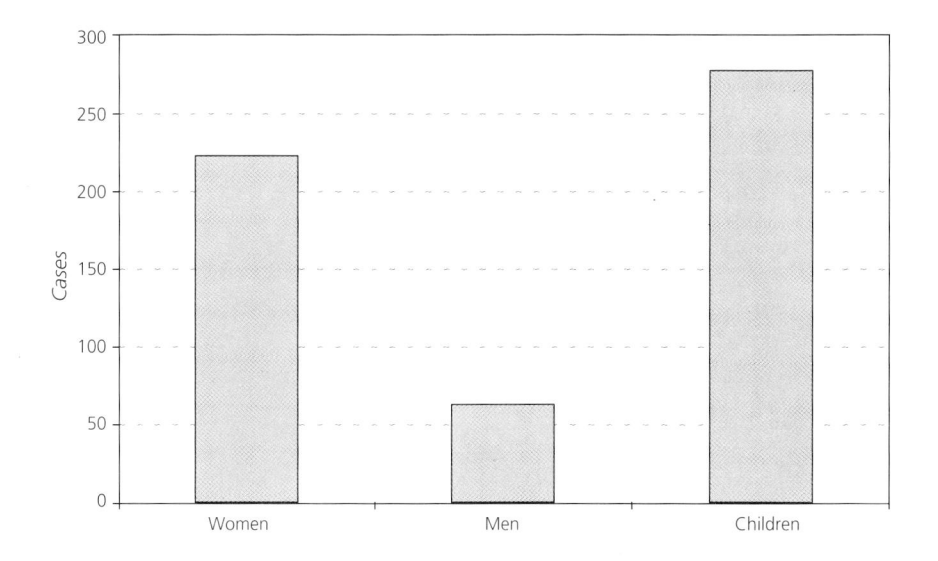

Mapping the Inhuman Trade

Figure VIII. Type of exploitation of women, men and children: percentage of cases including information on the type of exploitation

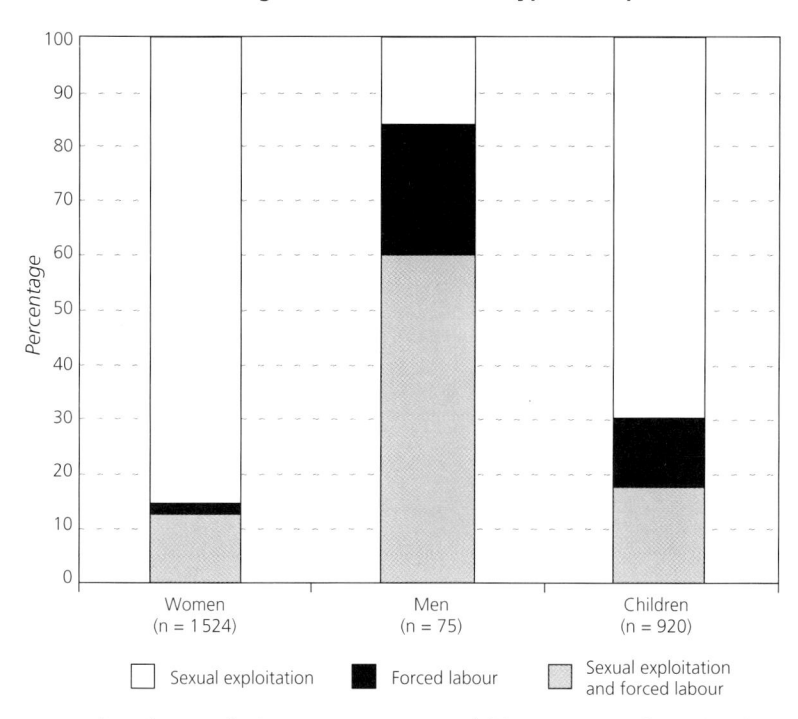

[Stacked bar chart showing percentages for Women (n = 1 524), Men (n = 75), and Children (n = 920), with categories: Sexual exploitation, Forced labour, Sexual exploitation and forced labour]

n = number of cases referring to women, men or children as victims of sexual exploitation or forced labour

Figure IX. Citations of trafficking involving sexual exploitation into a country, by region

(Percentage)

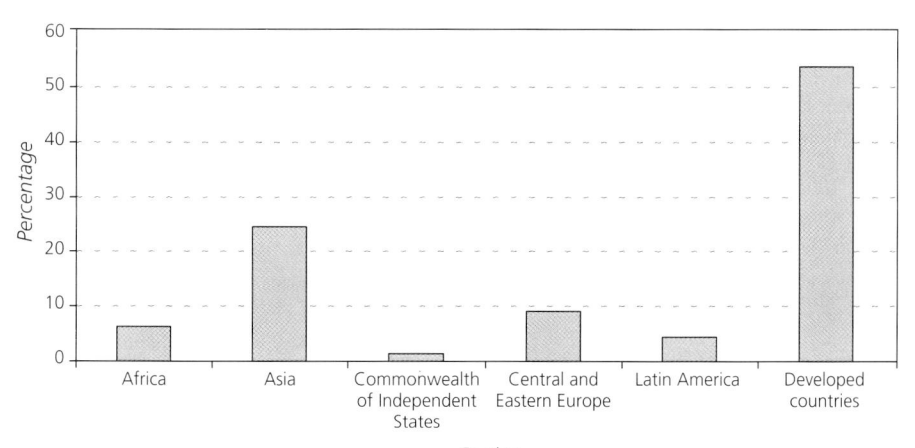

[Bar chart showing percentages by region: Africa, Asia, Commonwealth of Independent States, Central and Eastern Europe, Latin America, Developed countries]

Region

Figure X. Citations of trafficking involving forced labour into a country, by region

(Percentage)

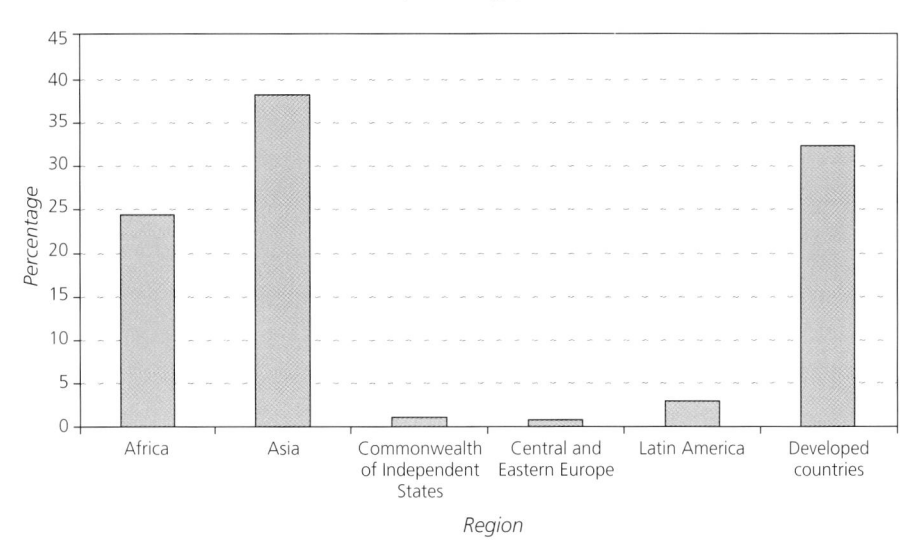

When exploitation patterns in countries to which persons are trafficked were viewed regionally, the picture became better defined. As can be seen in figure IX, sexual exploitation was most frequent in developed countries, followed by Asian countries. Exploitation through forced labour is more common in Asian countries, the developed world and African countries than in countries in other regions (figure X). However, it should be kept in mind that, in general, countries, especially the CIS member States and States in Latin America, were rarely mentioned as countries of destination, so their low numbers in relation to sexual exploitation and forced labour at the end of the trafficking process were to be expected.

Profile of the offender

Considerably less information can be found on offenders than on victims. Data on offenders included information about those who were suspected of being involved in trafficking as criminals and those who had been found guilty. As regards the nationality of offenders, a total of 76 countries were referred to as home countries of offenders. The countries most frequently referred to were the Russian Federation, Nigeria and Ukraine, in descending order:

Country	References[a]
Russian Federation	13
Nigeria	9
Ukraine	9
Albania	8
Thailand	7
Turkey	7
China	6
Poland	6
Bulgaria	5
Germany	5
Italy	5
Lithuania	5
Mexico	5
Romania	5

[a] Because of the low number of references the information should be treated with caution.

When the references to countries were examined from a regional perspective, it was noted that Asia had the highest number of references, followed by Central and Eastern Europe (see figure XI).

Figure XI. Number of references to the nationality of the offender, by region

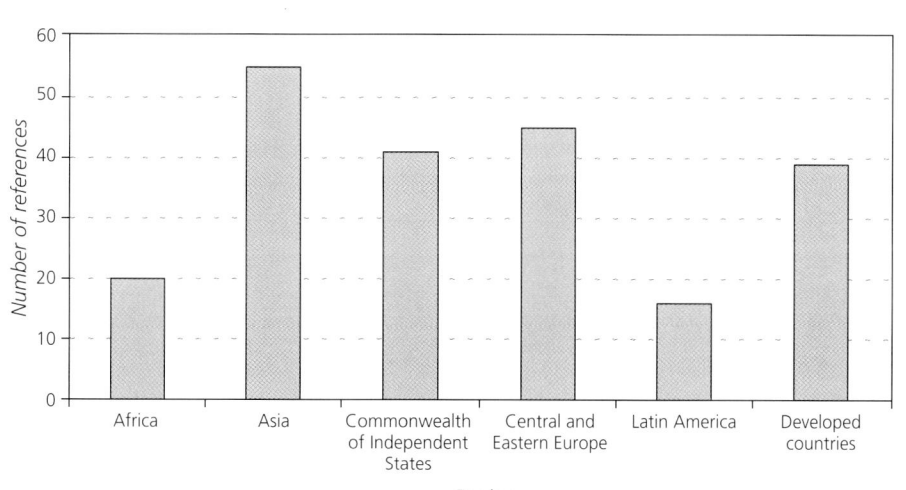

Conclusion

Even though there are a number of difficulties in collecting and analysing data on trafficking in human beings, the first results of the database of the United Nations Office on Drugs and Crime on human trafficking are encouraging. The systematic documentation of open-source data was able to yield information of importance for both policy purposes and theory formation.

Many results confirmed the received wisdom on human trafficking. Persons were typically recruited from poorer countries, transported through countries that provided geographically expedient and relatively safe routes and faced exploitation in more affluent parts of the world. The majority of victims were indeed, as expected, women and children and sexual exploitation was the most common form of exploitation, often combined with other forms. Obviously, then, trafficking in persons is a gender-specific phenomenon, reflecting the special vulnerabilities of women and girls in poor, post-conflict or badly governed countries. It constitutes a sad manifestation of the rampant violence against women and girls across the world against the backdrop of unmitigated gender inequalities in the global village.

Some specific new insights have been gained, such as that Central and Eastern Europe currently acts mainly as a transit area for trafficked persons and that Asia, even excluding Japan, is now as much a source as a destination region.

The results of the database can be used to set priorities for international cooperation. Special attention is due to countries that featured high in the rankings and where domestic capacity is still underdeveloped. A ranking of countries most in need of technical assistance seems feasible.

Trafficking profiles of the various regions and subregions showed great differences. Since different policies are required to tackle trafficking in origin, transit and destination countries, technical cooperation needs to be based on a sound understanding of the unique profile of the country, subregion or region in question. The database is a reliable source for that purpose.

As mentioned, this article presents preliminary findings. Some information could not yet be analysed at the present stage because sufficient data were not yet available. In the future, more data will be added, allowing more detailed analysis of different aspects of human trafficking.

Annex. Examples of collections of data on trafficking in human beings

The Protection Project at the Johns Hopkins University School of Advanced International Studies in Washington, D.C., has established a comprehensive database on human trafficking, which includes a collection of international conventions as well as domestic legislation that address issues of trafficking in persons; charts comparing the laws on trafficking for purposes of commercial sexual exploitation and other forms of slavery; a set of maps on legislative approaches and national and international trafficking routes, as well as other related information; over 50 testimonies of trafficking survivors; and updates on the status of investigations, prosecutions and convictions, as well as other stories, events and activities relevant to trafficking around the world. The Project publishes an annual *Human Rights Report on Trafficking in Persons, Especially Women and Children*, which includes a summary of laws and the scope of the trafficking problem in over 190 countries. The first report was published in March 2001 (www.protectionproject.org).

Based on the Trafficking Victims Protection Act of 2000, the Department of State of the United States of America has been mandated to submit an annual report on the status of severe forms of trafficking in persons in different countries. The first report was published in 2001 and the second in 2002. The report includes brief country narratives from 90 countries containing information on the trafficking situation and the Government's efforts to combat trafficking.[a]

The International Organization on Migration has established a database, which collects qualitative and quantitative information on trafficking victims assisted by the International Organization on Migration. The database includes data on numbers of victims assisted, their country of origin, age, trafficking route and the method in which they were trafficked.

The Innocenti Research Centre of the United Nations Children's Fund has initiated a data collection mainly on trafficking in children in African countries. The focus is on collecting quantitative and qualitative data on the phenomenon on action against trafficking in all African countries.

The Office for Democratic Institutions and Human Rights of the Organization for Security and Cooperation in Europe and the European Union have set up an online service, Legislationline. It compiles international texts and domestic legislation from its member States, including 55 countries in the Caucasus region, Central Asia,

---

[a]United States of America, Department of State, Under Secretary for Global Affairs, *Victims of Trafficking and Violence Protection Act of 2000: Trafficking in Persons Report* (Washington, D.C., 2002).

Europe and North America. It deals generally with the rule of law and the protection of human rights and fundamental freedoms and also includes trafficking legislation in many countries (see www.osce.org/odihr/).

Under the framework of the Task Force on Trafficking in Human Beings of the Stability Pact for South Eastern Europe, the Regional Clearing Point was established in order to ensure standardized regional data on victim assistance and protection, to support the further development of a network of shelters, and of national referral mechanisms throughout South Eastern Europe. The data collection has been initiated simultaneously in Albania, Bosnia and Herzegovina, Bulgaria, Croatia, the Republic of Moldova, Romania, Serbia and Montenegro (including Kosovo) and the former Yugoslav Republic of Macedonia (see www.osce.org/attf/).

References

1. Liz Kelly and Linda Regan, *Stopping Traffic: Exploring the Extent of, and Responses to, Trafficking in Women for Sexual Exploitation in the UK*, Police Research Series, Paper 125 (London, Home Office, 2000).
2. Alison Murray, "Debt-bondage and trafficking: don't believe the hype", *Global Sex Workers: Rights, Resistance and Redefinition*, Kamala Kempadoo and Jo Doezema, eds. (London/New York, Routledge, 1998), pp. 51-64.
3. John Salt, "Trafficking and human smuggling: a European perspective", *International Migration*, vol. 38, No. 3 (2000), pp. 31-54.
4. Frank Laczko, "Human trafficking: the need for better data", *Migration Information Source, Data Insights* (Washington, D.C., Migration Policy Institute, 2002), available at www.migrationinformation.org (accessed on 9 October 2003).
5. *Trafficking in Human Beings: First Report of the Dutch National Rapporteur* (The Hague, Bureau NRH, 2002).
6. International Organization for Migration, *Journeys of Jeopardy: a Review of Research on Trafficking in Women and Children in Europe*, IOM Migration Research Series, No. 11 (Geneva, 2002).
7. United Nations Office on Drugs and Crime and United Nations Interregional Crime and Justice Research Institute, *Coalitions against Trafficking in Human Beings in the Philippines: Research and Activities* (United Nations, New York, 2003).
8. Mark Shaw, Jan van Dijk and Wolfgang Rhomberg, "Determining global trends in crime and justice: an overview of results form the United Nations surveys of crime trends and operations of criminal justice systems", *Forum on Crime and Society*, vol. 3, Nos. 1-2 (2003).

9. Matti Joutsen, "Introduction", *Crime and Criminal Justice Systems in Europe and North America 1990-1994*, K. Kangaspunta, M. Joutsen and N. Ollus, eds., HEUNI publications No. 32 (Helsinki, European Institute for Crime Prevention and Control, affiliated with the United Nations, 1998).

10. Germany, Bundeskriminalamt, *Lagebild Menschenhandel* (Trafficking in human beings: situation report) (Wiesbaden, Germany, 1999, 2000 and 2001).

11. Sweden, National Criminal Investigation Department, National Criminal Intelligence Service, *Trafficking in Women: Situation Report*, Nos. 1-5 (Stockholm, 1998-2002).

12. Anna Alvazzi del Frate, "The voice of victims of crime: estimating the true level of conventional crime", *Forum on Crime and Society*, vol. 3, Nos. 1-2 (2003).

13. Frank Laczko, "Developing better indicators of trafficking: a review of some recent trends in Europe", paper presented to the second preparatory seminar for the eleventh Organization for Security and Co-operation in Europe Economic Forum, Ioannina, Greece, 17 and 18 February 2003.

14. Irena Omelaniuk, "Trafficking in persons: nature and logistics; case study—Balkans", presentation at the Conference on trafficking: networks and logistics of transnational organized crime and international terrorism, organized by the International Scientific and Professional Advisory Council, Courmayeur, Italy, 6-8 February 2002.

JUVENILE JUSTICE INITIATIVES IN LEBANON

by Alex Schmid* and Ralph Riachy**

Abstract

Outlining the five major phases in the field of juvenile justice in Lebanese legislation since 1943, the present article reviews the process of reform of the juvenile justice system in Lebanon, which has been supported by the United Nations Office on Drugs and Crime since 1999. The phenomenon of juvenile delinquency was previously poorly understood by the authorities, as shown by the measures of imprisonment, the length of preventive detention and the generally coercive regime in prisons. The main focus of the reform was on ensuring better conditions of detention and treatment of young offenders, attempting to prevent delinquency, ensuring educational assistance to young people in danger and protecting young victims. In order to achieve those aims, a Department for Minors has been set up in the Ministry of Justice. The Lebanese reform has to be seen as a small but significant step in the evolution of justice for juvenile offenders. A second project by the United Nations Office on Drugs and Crime will support the continuing process of reform.

INTRODUCTION

A country of 18 communities grouped into two large religious entities, Christian and Muslim, each one enjoying legislative and judiciary autonomy in the matter of personal status, Lebanon is an ethnic and cultural mosaic. In that context, the necessary reform of an outdated and ill-adapted system of justice for juvenile offenders proved to be a difficult but nevertheless achievable task. The present article provides a review of the reform process and, by implication, a number of lessons that can be learned from it.

Lebanese legislation in the field of justice for juvenile offenders has been marked by many phases; the five described below are perhaps the most important.

---

*Head of Project, Centre for International Crime Prevention, United Nations Office on Drugs and Crime, Beirut.
**President, Criminal Chamber, Court of Cassation, Beirut.

The Missed Step: the Penal Code of 1943

Compared with contemporary legislation on the subject, this phase, the Penal Code of 1943, given in particular the time period when it was implemented in Lebanon, was relatively advanced. It was characterized by provision for rehabilitation and reintegration measures and by the fact that judges were allowed to intervene in the course of application of those measures so as to modify or repeal them according to the interests of the minors concerned. In addition, a specialized jurisdiction for juvenile offenders was advocated and all coercive sentences were abolished. In reality, however, although the mechanisms provided for were perfect, the system lacked the ability to give them practical effect. Given the absence of specialized institutions, the lack of training and specialization of judges in the field, and the shortages as regards the necessary auxiliary personnel, the system could not achieve its objectives.

The Fall: the years 1948-1983

The return to a more rigid prison system became a reality with the abandonment of the innovative principles of the 1943 law and the development of a coercive regime based largely on sentences to be carried out in a secure environment. The rehabilitation measures so important in the 1943 Penal Code were no longer considered essential. In the context of a renewed outbreak of criminality driven by habitual offenders, rehabilitation measures were no longer felt to be necessary or appropriate.

The Rise: Article No. 119 of 16 September 1983

Article No. 119 of 16 September 1983 once again took up certain principles of the 1943 Penal Code, in particular those relating to rehabilitation, but without relinquishing the idea of sentences in a closed environment applying to juvenile offenders between the ages of 15 and 18.

Article No. 119 was chiefly characterized by the adoption of a legislative system for juvenile offenders that was no longer an integral part of the Penal Code. Although it did not return to the concept of specialized jurisdictions, the Article instituted the social worker as adviser to the judge in determining the sentence to be imposed. The most important provision of the Article was thus to introduce into the judicial function a role previously reserved for the social field.

Article No. 119 not only lacked a precise definition of rehabilitation measures, however, but details as to their content and the practical mechanics of their application were also not provided for. The protection of young people in danger was the subject of only one article, which proved to be confusing and difficult to apply. As a result, a reform of the system was warranted.

The Return: Law No. 422 of 6 July 2002

Established by the legislator with the assistance of national and international experts, Law No. 422 of 6 July 2002 was intended to respond to the imminent need for reform of the system.

The civil war from 1975 to 1990 had weakened critical economic, social and family structures. Lebanon was not in a position to confront the resulting escalation in juvenile delinquency without restructuring its legislative and institutional system in the area of juvenile justice.

As has already been stated, although earlier legislation provided for rehabilitation and reintegration measures, they were rarely applied; indeed, some were simply impossible to implement owing to the vagueness of their content. Furthermore, the absence of specialization among justice professionals, social workers and educators, as well as the lack of appropriate institutions aimed at reintegration, were key obstacles to taking up the challenge posed by juvenile delinquency.

Overall, the phenomenon and the implications of juvenile delinquency were poorly understood by the authorities responsible for the affairs of minors. Among other factors, this explains the popularity of imprisonment compared with educational and reintegration measures. Longer periods of preventive detention led to prison overpopulation in inappropriate facilities under the supervision of prison personnel with a lack of adequate training. In addition, the concept of protection of the young person in moral and physical danger was absent from judicial decisions.

The inadequacy of the system and Lebanon's ratification of the Convention on the Rights of the Child (General Assembly resolution 44/25, annex) made restructuring imperative. In response to a request from the national authorities, the United Nations Office on Drugs and Crime supported a concerted reform effort under a technical assistance project carried out from January 1999 to June 2002.

A review of juvenile delinquency in Lebanon

Key to the reform process was a detailed assessment of the position of juveniles in the Lebanese justice system. A thorough reading and analysis of the decisions of the courts between 1998 and 2000 shed light on the nature and spread of juvenile delinquency. One of the major results of this work was the growth in the number of minors presumed delinquent, taking into account the number of committed crimes reported by the judicial police and the number of dossiers reviewed annually by the courts. The results clearly indicated that the phenomenon remained essentially one of low-level delinquency and not of serious crime. Three quarters of the crimes reviewed were in fact less serious or petty offences.

Profile of the young people concerned

The data on delinquency reflect the image of the boy or young man as criminal offender. That situation is reinforced by a certain indulgence on the part of magistrates with regard to delinquent girls, given that there is an absence of centres of detention especially for girls, who are currently detained in prisons for women, as well as a sociocultural context that inhibits all disclosures that could affect family honour.

The average age of minors at the time of breaking the law was found to be mainly between 15 and 18. Nevertheless, there is an emerging tendency for younger offenders, in particular offenders between the ages of 12 and 15, to come into conflict with the law. This is illustrated in figure I below.

As regards the nationality of the offenders, children of Lebanese nationality represented the majority (60 per cent), followed by children of Syrian origin (20 per cent). A smaller proportion of the children (8 per cent) were of Palestinian origin.

At the time of committing the crime, the majority of minors had interrupted their schooling and found themselves already in the world of work. That situation explained the high level of illiteracy, the lack of any professional qualifications among young offenders and the fact that offenders were employed in activities producing irregular or unstable incomes.

Nature of the crimes committed by minors

Delinquency appears above all to be directed against property, often as a means of survival. The crime most frequently committed by minors is theft.

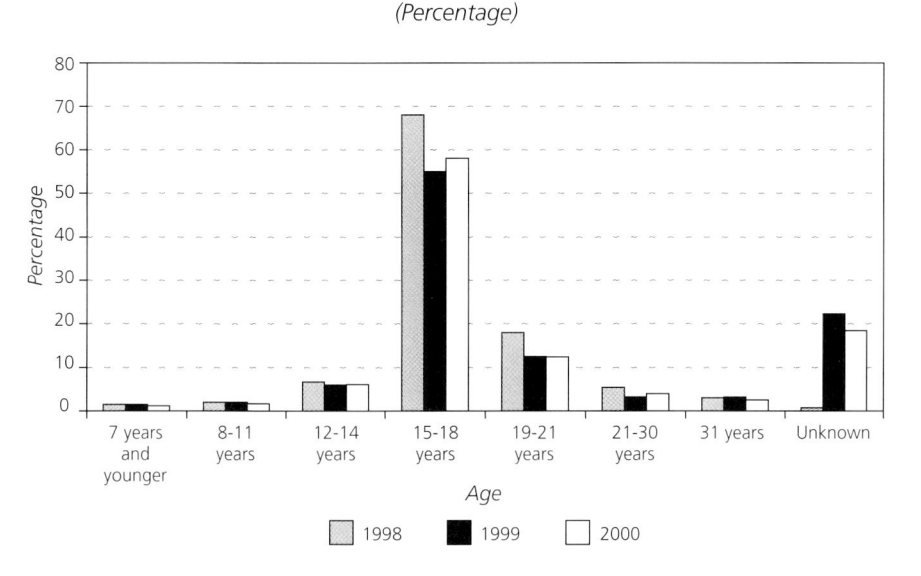

Figure I. Age at the time of committing the crime, 1998-2000

(Percentage)

As regards manner of execution of crimes, whether in a group, with other minors, with adults or family members or alone (see figure II), committing a crime as an individual indicates an impulsive tendency without premeditation and 75 per cent of crimes committed by minors took that form. However, a renewed growth of the "gang" phenomenon has been noted and the increased level of participation by adults in crimes committed by minors raises the issue of exploitation of minors by adults for criminal profit.

Sentencing

Prison remains the standard response, regardless of the gravity of the crime committed. Prison sentences were pronounced in 35 per cent of cases in 2000, while probation was provided for in only 6.4 per cent of cases, re-education in 6.3 per cent and various protection measures in 3.8 per cent of cases (see figure III).

Prison sentences are usually of short duration, that is, of less than two months, a period in which no activities or programmes of rehabilitation can be realistically or effectively carried out.

As regards probationary and protective measures, they are only rarely resorted to owing to the lack of personnel with the professional qualifications required and the absence of the necessary structures for application and follow-up.

Figure II. Distribution of crimes according to the manner of execution, 1998-2000

(Percentage)

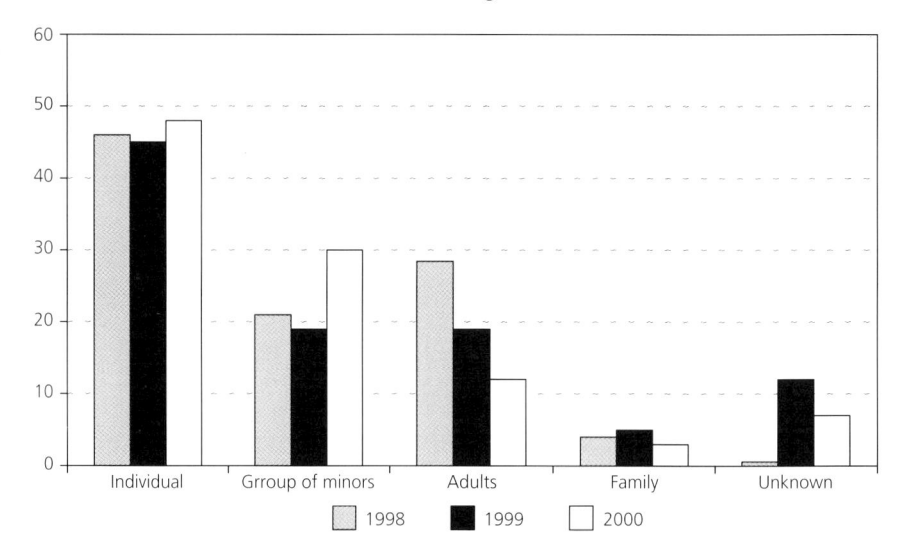

Figure III. Measures and sentences pronounced by the juvenile court

(Percentage)

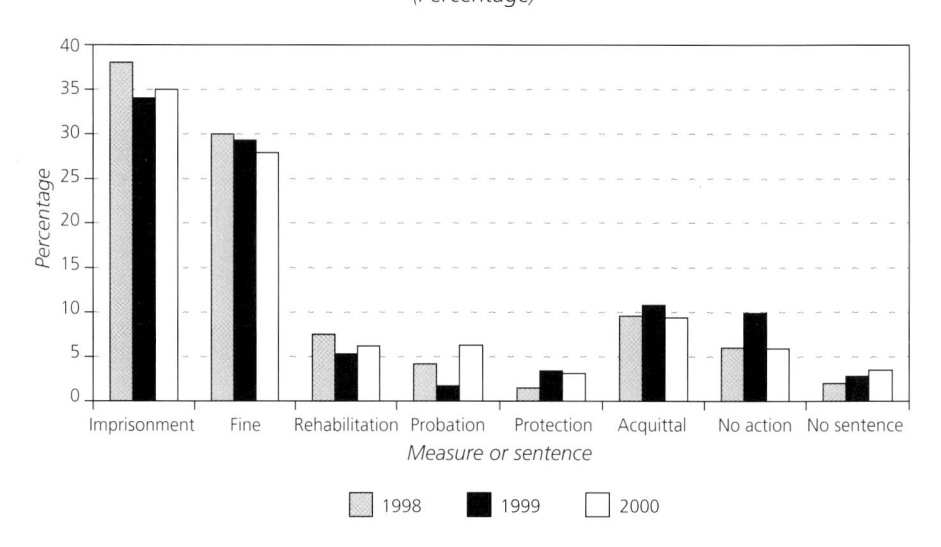

The reform process: achievements and first assessment

Character of the reform

Although the majority of cases of delinquency concern minor offences, the solution most often resorted to has been an increase in repression. That approach has often resulted in inappropriate sentences, thus ironically increasing the risks of recidivism. The emphasis now, however, is on encouraging measures of social protection for young offenders before they slide into delinquency. In addition, it is now considered necessary to treat not only the crime itself but above all the actions of the offender as the symptom of a social shortcoming in need of correction. The concept of the interest of the child thus constitutes an essential element of the reform process.

The reforms have aimed to endow the justice system with the means to balance the requirement to punish with ensuring the protection, the well-being and the rights of minors who enter into conflict with the law. In addition, key concepts include preventing delinquency through judicial measures and providing educational assistance to young people in danger, as well as ensuring the protection of victims who are minors.

Elements of the reform: legislative matters

In adopting Law No. 422 of 6 July 2002, legislators were aiming to respond in an adequate manner to the interests of minors and to ensure the pre-eminence of protection, education and rehabilitation measures.

Law No. 422 is characterized by the statement of certain fundamental principles that are key to its interpretation. Article 2 declares, for example, the supreme importance of the interests of juvenile offenders and the need for an autonomous procedure to deal with them where alternative forms of sentencing and rehabilitation are the norm. In contrast, confinement or imprisonment is regarded as a measure to be applied only in exceptional circumstances.

The Law expanded the range of measures available to the courts as sentences for juveniles and outlined them in a precise manner, providing a clear methodology for their application. In line with its objective of rehabilitating the minor in his or her home environment, the Law provided for a range of measures, including reprimands, protection, "monitored freedom" and work of general interest or reparation for the victim. Those measures may be modified by the judge during the course of their application.

Although the Law reduced sentences in exceptional cases for offenders aged 15-18 who had committed serious crimes, such sentences were counterbalanced by the power given to judges to defer execution of sentences or to replace them with rehabilitation measures where the offender was not deprived of his or her freedom.

Although the Law retained the possibility of preventive detention, it restricted its application to certain crimes and under precise conditions. Detention, which can only be carried out in a suitable place, is contingent upon the preparation of a social and medical dossier after the submission of the juvenile offender to a physical and psychological examination.

In addition, the Law provided for exhaustive protective arrangements for juvenile offenders in particular danger of recidivism. Such measures can either be decided by the judge or at the request of the young offender himself. Increases in the number of homeless minors, often engaged in begging and vagrancy, justified such measures.

In order to strengthen the role of social and educational personnel, the social worker has become the principal actor in the administration of justice for juvenile offenders. The presence of the social worker throughout the proceedings, from the preliminary inquiries to the reintegration phase, is now required by law.

In order to ensure effective application of the Law, the importance of the Department for Minors of the Ministry of Justice has been underlined, in particular its function as coordinating office between the different services and the organizations concerned.

From the moment of its entry into force on 13 July 2002, the effects of the Law have been evident. Limitation of the use of detention has led to a reduction in the number of minors detained in the juvenile wing of the central prison of Roumieh, in Beirut. As a point of comparison, in July 2001, 219 minors were in detention, whereas in July 2002 there were only 147, a figure that is all the more significant in view of the fact that during the annual holidays from July to September there is usually an increase in petty criminal activity and a consequent increase in the number of detainees. The reduced use of preventive detention in 2002 compared with the previous two years is illustrated in figure IV.

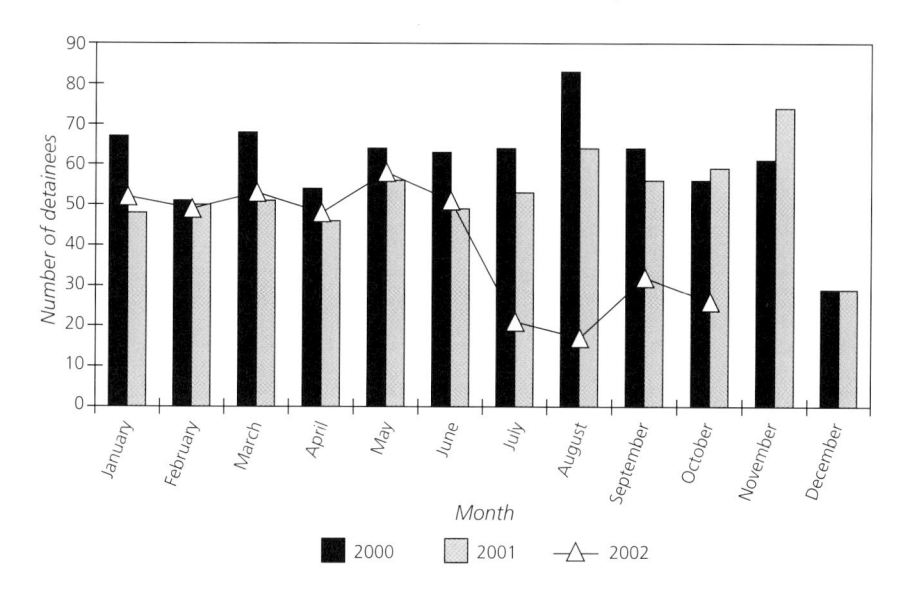

Figure IV. Detention of juvenile offenders by month, 2000-2002

Institutional reforms

As already mentioned, one of the essential elements of the reform in Lebanon was the establishment of the Department for Minors as part of the Ministry of Justice. The Department is responsible, in cooperation with other concerned ministries, for the development of new initiatives within the framework of social reintegration. In addition, the Ministry is responsible for establishing reintegration programmes and for developing plans of action to prevent juvenile delinquency and to protect young people.

The Department, within which a computerized system of data related to delinquency has been established, has provided the necessary opportunity to both systematize best practice concerning juvenile offenders and to support the activities of professionals responsible for various aspects of the administration of justice to minors. The database will assist in evaluating the impact of the reforms on the system of juvenile justice as a whole.

The establishment of a supervisory role for social workers has resulted in an increase in the number of these professionals being present during the questioning of minors by police officers, which is indeed now obligatory under the reform programme. The impact of the new policy on ensuring the presence of social workers during interrogations is illustrated in figure V.

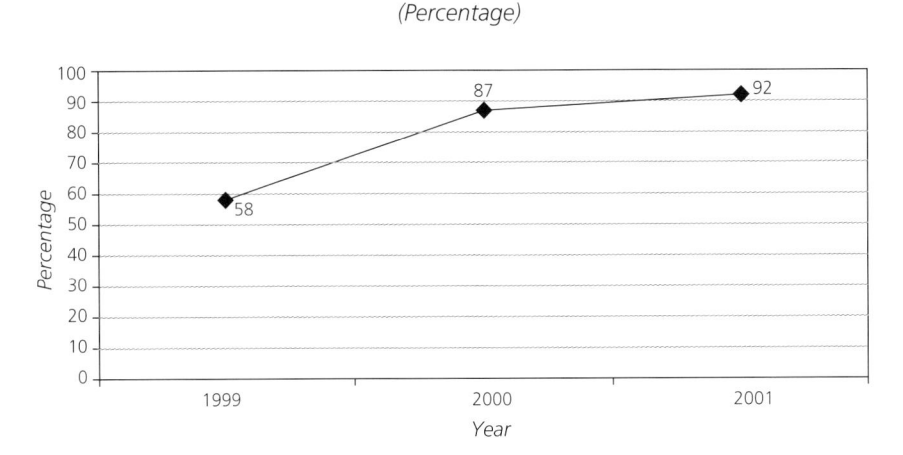

Figure V. Presence of social workers during questioning of minors, 1999-2000

(Percentage)

[Line chart showing: 1999: 58%, 2000: 87%, 2001: 92%]

A number of other institutional measures have also been taken to ensure the effective implementation of the reform programme, including the establishment of a special police unit, the Minors Brigade, responsible for questioning delinquent minors and taking statements from young victims. In addition, a reorganization of the system of information about juvenile offenders has been critical in ensuring that the correct information is available at every phase of the judicial process, thus making quicker judicial decisions possible.

Prison reform

A process of reform of the conditions of detention and the treatment of juvenile offenders has been initiated with a view to adapting the national situation to the United Nations Rules for the Protection of Juveniles deprived of their Liberty (General Assembly resolution 45/113, annex) and to the Convention on the Rights of the Child.

The activities in this area aim:

(a) To establish a coordination unit within the juvenile wing of Beirut Prison responsible for centralizing data concerning the status of juvenile offenders and for providing the necessary information to social workers and magistrates;

(b) To refurbish and reconstruct prisons and places of detention for juvenile offenders in order to ensure an improvement in the living conditions of detainees;

(c) To reorganize academic, educational and professional activities in order to improve the process of social rehabilitation of offenders;

(d) To set up a new centre for the rehabilitation of juvenile offenders.

The establishment of new standardized dossiers that bring together the information required at all stages of the judicial process and the computerization and management of dossiers within the prison have made it possible to reduce considerably the time taken for judicial procedures to run their course. The reduction in the length of detention of young offenders has been one of the most important results, as illustrated in figure VI.

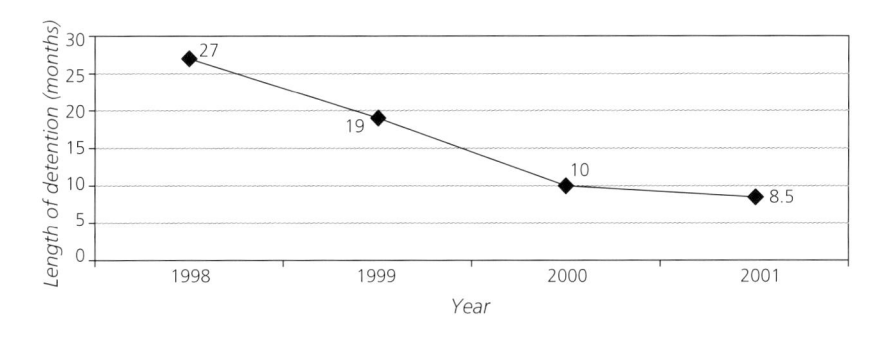

Figure VI. Average length of detention of juvenile offenders, 1998-2000
(Months)

Year	Length of detention (months)
1998	27
1999	19
2000	10
2001	8.5

Training of professionals

In order to perform their functions effectively, the professionals in charge of the affairs of juvenile offenders should have knowledge of and special training in working with children and adolescents. Professional specialization constitutes an essential element in ensuring the impartial and efficient administration of justice for minors with particular focus on the well-being of young offenders themselves.

A series of training activities have been initiated, focusing on the application of arrangements relating to conciliation procedures, educational measures, alternative sentencing, treatment and rehabilitation of delinquents and the prevention of delinquency. As a result, it has been possible to train a growing number of professionals. This training has become an obligatory part of the core curriculum for legal professionals. It is also available to persons who wish to specialize or who already exercise specific functions in the field, such as social workers, police officers and prison personnel.

Conclusion

A reform of the justice system is an expression of the evolution of sociocultural concepts in the environment in which they apply and the progression of the reform process itself serves the further advancement of those concepts. The Lebanese experience of reform has been a small step in the evolution of justice for juvenile offenders and has contributed to an improvement in conditions for children and adolescents in the country. Efforts should be continued to ensure that the system of justice for young offenders is an integral part of improved social justice for children and young people. The success of the initial reform efforts is being built upon by a second project being carried out by the United Nations Office on Drugs and Crime that seeks, among other things, to continue the reform of prisons and conditions of detention for girls; to establish social programmes for the prevention of recidivism; and to establish a procedure for the judicial protection of victims who are minors.

Reforming the justice system in a multi-ethnic society remains a key challenge. The experience gained in Lebanon can be of great value to others making similar efforts.

CRIMINAL VICTIMIZATION IN FOUR MAJOR CITIES IN SOUTHERN INDIA

by K. Chockalingham*

Abstract

Victimization surveys are an important source of reliable information as a basis for understanding and combatting national and local crime, in particular in developing countries such as India where the quality and reliability of official crime reports are questionable. This said, victims and their problems have been the subject of serious research for the past 20 years in India. The present paper analyses one of the first victim surveys carried out in the State of Tamil Nadu, in southern India. It focuses on three main areas: the extent of criminal victimization, the reporting behaviour of victims and victims' perceptions of police performance. A number of conclusions are drawn: firstly, that many crimes in India go unreported; secondly, that the crimes that are more likely to be reported are cases where there is material loss or damage; and finally, that victims are generally unsatisfied with police performance.

INTRODUCTION

To understand crime levels, three standard sources of crime data are generally used: official crime reports, self-reports and victim surveys. Crime reports generated by criminal justice agencies contain different information, depending on the requirements of the registering agency. Police reports cannot be considered an accurate account of the number of crimes perpetrated as not all crimes are reported by victims, not all police calls are determined to be crimes that should be registered and not all police departments underscore the importance of crime reports.

Because of the variety of recording practices, practical problems and political agendas, crime statistics just reflect the police performance in recording crimes [1]. The nature of reporting of crime varies from country to country, depending on the type of crime. According to some estimates, the general ratio between crimes actually committed and crimes made known to the police is quite high, crimes being made known to the police

---
*Professor of Criminology, Criminal Law and Victimology, and Vice-Chancellor, Manomaniam Sundaranar University, Tirunelveli, Tamil Nadu, India

constituting between 30 and 40 per cent of all those committed. For some offences, such as assaults and sexual offences, the ratio is much lower, 1 to 10 or less. One general rule of thumb is that, the more serious the offence, the lower the "dark" figure of unreported crime, although even this is not always the case [2]. In many police forces there exists a rule of not recording crimes that do not meet a minimum standard of seriousness [3].

In India, the National Crime Records Bureau collects crime data from the police headquarters of all the states across the country and has a system to standardize the data it receives. It categorizes the reports mainly into offences against the person and offences against property. These constitute the official crime statistics published annually.

Another form of assessing the volume of crime in any society is by interviewing the victims of crime. Victimization surveys help to elicit a clearer picture of levels of criminal victimization as well as the opinion of a cross-section of society on matters relating to crime and punishment, their perception of the criminal justice agencies and the method of handling of offenders and victims. The information collected from victims also covers their experience before, during and after the offence has occurred.

International crime victim surveys

Over the past 20 years, a growing number of countries have initiated victimization surveys to assess national or local crime problems. Such surveys ask representative samples of the general public about selected offences they may have experienced over a given time. The resulting victimization rates constitute a better indicator of the level of crime than the number of crimes reported to and recorded by the police. If the research methodology used is standardized, surveys also offer a new opportunity for the collection of crime statistics that can be used for cross-country comparative purposes. The International Crime Victim Survey (ICVS) was initiated in 1987 with that in mind. The essence of these surveys is that crime is not studied from the perspective of state agencies but from that of the public at large. Respondents can inform the researchers about what they perceive to be criminal victimization, regardless of state policies. They can also provide information about their dealings with state agencies in relation to those experiences [4]. Apart from identifying crime trends, victim surveys indicate broad areas for further debate, investigation and intervention [5].

Victim surveys in India

In India, the study of victims and their problems has been taken up by researchers in a serious way only in the last 20 years [6]. Despite the fact that law enforcement officers and social scientists in India have been admitting in academic and other forums that the actual volume of crime is considerably greater than what is reported in the official crime statistics, no victimization survey has been conducted in that country with the exception of one in Mumbai in 1992. One of the recommendations of the victim survey conducted in Mumbai was that victimization surveys must be conducted on a regular basis in order to obtain a more precise index of crime [7]. The study on which the present article is based is therefore one of the first victim surveys in India, attempting to record not only a comprehensive pictures of crime but also citizens' perceptions of the agencies of criminal justice.

The locale of the study, the State of Tamil Nadu, is situated in the southern part of the Indian peninsula, with Chennai as its capital. The study forms part of a major project funded by the University Grants Commission, New Delhi [8].

The main objectives of the study were threefold: firstly, to understand the extent of criminal victimization in the State of Tamil Nadu; secondly, to study the reporting behaviour of victims of various crimes; and finally, to analyse the opinion of victims on the performance of the police.

Methodology

Research questions were framed to meet the objectives of the study. A pre-coded interview schedule, similar to the one used in the International Crime Victim Survey, supplemented by certain questions relevant to the Indian setting, was constructed by the researcher. The respondents were contacted by the investigators and asked to respond to the interview based on their victimization in the last five years.

Four major cities in Tamil Nadu—Madurai, Coimbatore, Trichy and Chennai—were chosen for the study. Using random sampling, administrative units in each city were chosen. The streets in each of those administrative units were then selected randomly and the household—the basic sampling unit for the study—was randomly selected from the list of door numbers.

Demographic data and sample characteristics

While the city of Chennai is populated mainly by upper and middle-class citizens, the other three cities consist mainly of people who belong to the middle and lower classes. Two factors that determine that composition are occupation and the cost of living. Some 73 per cent of the sample population in the study were middle class in terms of their residential status. A major part of the remaining sample was from the upper class (12 per cent). The majority of the respondents lived in houses (43 per cent) or flats (56 per cent). The household size was mainly within the range of 3-4 members (47 per cent) and 5-6 persons (36 per cent). Some 63 per cent of the families had 3-4 adult members (47 per cent), that is members above 16 years of age, and 16 per cent of families had 5-6 adult members, with 18 per cent having 1-2 adult members in their families.

The majority of the 4,030 respondents were in the age groups of 16-20 years (21 per cent) and 26-30 years (16 per cent). Nearly half the sample was concentrated in the 16-30 year age group. The sample consisted of a majority of males (62 per cent), 54 per cent of them married and 40 per cent single. In terms of level of education, the sample consisted mainly of college (51 per cent) and secondary school (30 per cent) graduates. Very few had higher education, that is, a postgraduate or other university degree (3 per cent). A majority of the respondents were working (41 per cent) and the remainder were students (26 per cent). All the respondents selected for the interview agreed to participate in the survey. The selected sample, in terms of gender, age and education, appear to be an appropriate representative sample in the case of each city.

It should be noted that, while the survey asked respondents to identify when they had been victimized, the resulting data should not always be regarded as reliable, given that the exact timing of incidents (in particular of less serious ones) was not always easy to recall.

The nature and extent of victimization

Vehicle thefts and related crimes

Only 6 per cent of the total sample owned cars; among these, 5 per cent had been victims of car theft within the last five years. In comparison with car theft, the number of incidents of theft from cars was remarkably high (27 per cent). Damage of cars was also high, with 9 per cent of those who owned cars having been subjected to car vandalism.

As most of the sample came from middle-class families, ownership of two-wheelers was nearly eight times (53 per cent) the ownership of four-wheel motor vehicles. Only about 4 per cent of the respondents who owned two-wheelers had been subjected to moped thefts, mostly in the years before 1998 (46 per cent). Nearly three quarters of the sample surveyed (72 per cent) owned bicycles. Of those, 9 per cent had been victims of bicycle theft, the majority before the year 1998 (46 per cent).

Interestingly, there exists a correlation between the education level of the victims and the risks of victimization: none of the uneducated were victims of bicycle theft. This indicates that the poorest members of the population take extreme care to protect their possessions, as the bicycle is their only mode of transport.

Burglary, robbery and personal theft

If the numbers of victimizations for burglary, attempted burglary, robbery and personal theft in the sample population are examined, 4 per cent have been victims of burglary, 3 per cent of attempted burglary, 2 per cent of robbery and 10 per cent victims of personal theft. In the majority of each of those crimes, except for personal theft, the maximum number of victimizations occurred prior to the year 1998. The majority of the personal theft cases were victims of pickpocketing. There was no significant difference between victimization by attempted burglary and the status of the residential area of the respondent.

Sexual offences and assaults or threats

Two per cent of the total sample population had been victims of sexual offences, with 56 per cent having been victims during the year 1999. Two per cent of the respondents were victims of assault or threat, the majority in the years 1999 (39 per cent) and 1998 (31 per cent).

The majority of victims had had secondary or college education. More specifically, a chi-square analysis shows the existence of a correlation between victimization by sexual offences and the educational status of the victims. The majority of the sexual abuse victims were school and college students (45 per cent). The higher incidence of sexual victimization of students could be due to the fact that they all travelled during peak hours by public transport and also that their age made them more vulnerable. In the majority of the sexual offence cases, the offenders were single (52 per cent) and not known to the victim (61 per cent). The nature of the sexual offence was offensive behaviour in more than half of the cases (67 per cent) and indecent assault in 20 per cent of cases. A large majority of the victims (80 per cent) accepted the incident as a crime. In 46 per cent of the cases the victims were only threatened and in 32 per cent actual force was used. Weapons were used in 25 per cent of the cases, mostly weapons other than knives (34 per cent). Fewer than a quarter of the victims reported that they had been injured during the assault (15 per cent); 11 individuals had been injured gravely enough to seek medical assistance.

Consumer fraud and corruption

Significantly, victims of consumer fraud and corruption constituted 27 per cent and 26 per cent respectively of the total survey sample. More than half of the victims in the case of consumer frauds (55 per cent) had been cheated by shops; 14 per cent had been cheated by hotels and restaurants. About 13 per cent of victims had been cheated in consumer durable sales outlets by reduced weights, decreased quality of product and fake products. Just over half of the respondents (59 per cent), who had been victims of corruption had been victimized by government officials, 18 per cent having been victimized by police officers.

Interestingly, there is no significant correlation between victimization by corruption and the status of the residential area of the victim. However, nearly 75 per cent of the victims were from middle-class residential areas. In contrast, only 13 per cent of the residents of upper-class areas had been victims of corruption. At least one reason for this breakdown is the fact that members of the middle class usually approach government departments directly to get work done or for favours. In contrast, members of the upper class usually get such "business" done through their subordinates or mediators.

There is a significant difference between victimization by corruption and the level of education of the victim. The study revealed that the majority of those who had been victimized were college (40 per cent) and secondary school educated (35 per cent). It is perhaps surprising that 10 per cent of the victims had received some form of higher or university education and that almost all the victims of corruption had a relatively high level of education.

Reporting behaviour

Vehicle thefts and related crimes

Predictably, reporting behaviour was very high for vehicle theft, with more than three quarters of the victims of car theft (76 per cent) and moped theft (72 per cent) reporting the crime to the police. For theft from cars, non-reporting on the part of the victims occurred in only half the cases reported to the victim survey (43 per cent).

While car theft was considered very serious by a large majority of the victim sample, it is surprising that 15 per cent considered it fairly serious and the remainder a not very serious offence (8 per cent). Theft from cars, on the other hand, was considered a very serious incident only by 22 per cent of the victims. Car vandalism was considered a fairly serious offence by half of the victims, while nearly a quarter considered it as very serious (20 per cent). Moped theft was considered a serious offence by half of the victims, a quarter considering it very serious. More than 50 per cent of the victims of bicycle theft viewed it only as a fairly serious incident (62 per cent). This probably explains the corresponding high percentages in the reporting of those offences.

Burglary, attempted burglary, robbery and theft

According to the data for the reporting behaviour of the victims of offences such as burglary, attempted burglary, robbery and personal theft, the percentage of non-reporting was extremely high, for the crime of personal theft (79 per cent), burglary (48 per cent) and robbery (58 per cent). A majority of the victims of robbery (38 per cent), attempted burglary (43 per cent) and personal theft (62 per cent) stated that they regarded the incident as fairly serious, while 28 per cent regarded the offence of robbery as very serious. This is an important finding as it suggests that, despite the degree of seriousness with which an offence is regarded, victims think of reporting a crime only when there is actual loss of or damage to their property.

Sexual offences and assaults or threats

Reporting behaviour on the part of the victims of sexual offences and victims of assault or threat was poor. Only 4 per cent of the victims of sexual offences and 24 per cent of assault victims had reported the crimes to the police. For a majority of sexual crime victims (64 per cent), the incident was fairly serious and for 28 per cent and 54 per cent of the assault victims the incident was regarded as very serious and fairly serious, respectively.

Consumer fraud and corruption

Non-reporting in the case of consumer fraud and corruption cases occurred in nearly 100 per cent of cases. In consumer fraud cases the reporting was less than 1 per cent, with this being the same in the case of corruption. Such behaviour is partly the result of fear on the part of citizens or consumers that they will incur the displeasure of officials and will have to face the consequences in future dealings with government and/or commercial organizations. There is a significant correlation between the level of education and the reporting of corruption cases, with respondents with higher levels of education being more likely to report such cases to the authorities.

Perceptions of police performance

Satisfaction by crime type

Among all the offences covered, levels of dissatisfaction with police performance appeared to be the highest among burglary victims (54 per cent) followed by the assault or threat victims (52 per cent).

On the whole, the victims of crimes such as theft from cars, burglary, robbery, sexual offences and assault or threat who were not satisfied with the police attributed this to the police not doing enough to find the offender and recover their goods. All the victims of theft from cars were dissatisfied with the police because they had failed to recover their lost property. Burglary victims, besides the other reasons already mentioned, also felt that the police had not kept them informed about any progress being made in the case. Similarly, 20 per cent of the robbery victims also felt that the police had not kept them properly informed about the case. Improper treatment by the police (although the form this took was unspecified) was one of the most significant reasons for dissatisfaction with the police by the assault or threat victims (75 per cent).

Perceptions of crime levels

As regard the opinion of the respondents on solidarity in their neighbourhood—defined broadly as to whether people in a given area help each other or go their own way—39 per cent said that generally they assisted fellow citizens who lived in their area. Interestingly, the majority of the respondents were from the city of Madurai (29 per cent), followed closely by Chennai (25 per cent) and Coimbatore (24 per cent). It should be noted, however, that 19 per cent of all respondents in the survey stated that they mostly went their way without attempting to assist their fellows.

Perceptions of local policing

Thirty-six per cent of the sample population expressed the view that the police did a good job in controlling crime, while 42 per cent were of the view that the police performed poorly.

There were, however, important differences, depending on the city of origin, among those who said the police did a good job in controlling crime: 41 per cent were from Trichy, 25 per cent from Madurai and 21 per cent from Coimbatore. In contrast, only 11 per cent in Chennai felt the same. Whatever the differences, however, less than half of the persons in the sample were happy with police performance in all four cities. In Coimbatore and Chennai in particular, the percentage of satisfaction was very low compared with the other cities. Since they are large cities in comparison with Madurai and Trichy, police public interaction is probably less and therefore there are higher levels of dissatisfaction with the police for failing to control levels of crime.

Of the total sample, only 18 per cent said that police patrolling by car or by foot was done once a day; 11 per cent believed that it was done once a week, 19 per cent that it is done only once a month, 14 per cent less often and 22 per cent never, while 11 per cent did not know how often patrolling was done in their area.

Conclusion

The figures drawn from the analysis make it quite clear that many crimes occurring in India are not reported and that police figures are only the tip of the iceberg. Not all crimes are reported, but when they are, victims are more often than not dissatisfied with police performance. Overall, reporting behaviour depends largely on the value of loss incurred and the seriousness of the offence. Crime prevention does not just mean recording the occurrence of crime and increasing patrolling in the area for a period of time. What is necessary for crime control is analysing opportunities for criminals and studying victim-related issues such as the nature and extent of victimization, relationships between offenders and their victims, reporting behaviour and other factors. This is where victim surveys play a significant role. The need to conduct victim surveys is particularly apparent in developing countries such as India, where the quality of police recording of crime is questionable.

References

1. M. Shaw, J. van Dijk and W. Rhomberg, "Determining trends in global crime and justice: an overview of results from the United Nations surveys of crime trends and operations of criminal justice systems", *Forum on Crime and Society*, vol. 3, Nos. 1-2 (2003.)

2. Anna Alvazzi del Frate, *Victims of Crime in the Developing World*, UNICRI publication No. 57 (Rome, United Nations Interregional Crime and Justice Research Institute, 1998).

3. J. J. M. van Dijk, *The Victim's Willingness to Report to the Police: a Function of Prosecution Policy?* (The Hague Ministry of Justice of the Netherlands, 1979).

4. J. J. M. van Dijk, "Criminal victimization and victim empowerment in international perspective", *Caring for Crime Victims: Selected Proceedings of the 9th International Symposium on Victimology*, J. J. M. van Dijk, R. E. H. van Kaan and J. Wemmers, eds. (New York, Criminal Justice Press, 1999).

5. Antoinette Louw and others, *Crime in Johannesburg: Results of a City Victim Survey*, ISS Monograph Series, No. 18 (Johannesburg, South Africa, Institute for Security Studies, 1998).

6. K. Chockalingam, "A review of victimological developments in India", *Japanese Journal of Victimology*, vol. 3, No. 20 (1995), pp. 78-95.

7. D. R. Singh, "The International Crime (Victim) Survey in Bombay", *Criminal Victimization in the Developing World*, UNICRI Publication No. 55 (Rome, United Nations Interregional Crime and Justice Research Institute, 1995), pp. 95-134.

8. K. Chockalingam, "Victimization survey in four major cities in Tamil Nadu", unpublished major research project report funded by the University Grants Commission, New Delhi, December 2001.

THE VOICE OF VICTIMS OF CRIME: ESTIMATING THE TRUE LEVEL OF CONVENTIONAL CRIME

by Anna Alvazzi del Frate*

Abstract

Since its launch in 1989, the International Crime Victim Survey has attracted growing interest from the research community and policy makers. In addition to providing an alternative source of data on crime to complement official statistics, the Survey offers internationally standardized indicators for the perception and fear of crime. At the country level, the International Crime Victim Survey is used to monitor differences in crime and perceptions between countries and over time. By collecting social and demographic information on respondents, crime surveys also allow analysis of how both objective and subjective risks of crime vary for different groups within the population, in terms of age, gender, education, income levels and lifestyles. Data from recent sweeps of the Survey are presented in order to analyse global crime levels and trends.

INTRODUCTION

The main objectives of the International Crime Victim Survey include:

- Providing comparative indicators of crime and victimization risks, indicators of perception of crime and fear of crime, performance of law enforcement, victim assistance and crime prevention
- Promoting crime surveys as an important research and policy tool at the international, national and local levels
- Enhancing adequate research and policy analysis methodology
- Creating an opportunity for transparency in public debate about crime and reactions to crime
- Encouraging public and criminal justice concern about citizens' participation in the evaluation of criminal policy and particularly in partnership in crime prevention
- Promoting international cooperation by providing an opportunity for a large number of countries to share methodology and experience through their participation in a well coordinated international research project

---

*Crime Prevention and Criminal Justice Officer, United Nations Office on Drugs and Crime.

The International Crime Victim Survey shares with national crime surveys the objective of measuring crime beyond the information provided by police statistics. Indeed, one of the most important aspects of the Survey is its ability to measure the quantity of crime that is not reported to the police. The reasons for the non-reporting of crimes have to do with the inaccessibility of the authorities, which makes reporting difficult, complicated reporting procedures and a lack of confidence that reporting victimization to the police will result in solving the crime or punishing the perpetrator. Such measurements of unreported crime demonstrate that reports of official crime levels as outlined by Shaw, van Dijk and Rhomberg [1] provide only part of the picture and that citizens' elementary right of access to justice, and that of victims to be heard and protected are not met. This is particularly true in developing countries and countries with economies in transition and among vulnerable groups such as women and children.

The study of corruption, including "street-level corruption" and the perception of corruption among the general population, is an important and unique feature of the Survey. The perception of corruption can be monitored over time and compared with an objective measure.

Participation in the Survey has been facilitated by the international community and donors who have taken an interest in and supported the reform process towards a market economy and a democratic political system. It is, however, important to repeat the collection of data on a regular basis. The fifth "sweep" of the Survey is planned for 2004.

Overview of the international crime victim survey, 1989-2002

Initially called the International Crime Survey, the International Crime Victim Survey was carried out for the first time in 14 developed countries in 1989. Subsequently, in 1992, a face-to-face interview for the questionnaire was developed to enable the participation of countries in which telephone interviews would not have been feasible at the time. From that time, it became possible to conduct standardized surveys on crime in a number of countries for which very little information on crime was available. The third Survey was conducted in 1996 and the fourth in 2000; the project now includes more than 70 countries, all of which have participated in the survey at least once. The fourth Survey was carried out in 2000 and included 17 national surveys and 31 city surveys (16 capital cities in Central and Eastern Europe, 4 in Asia, 7 in Africa and 4 in Latin America). (For a detailed list of survey participants, see table.)

Countries and territories that participated in the International Crime Victim Survey at least once, 1989-2002

(N = national survey; C = city survey)

Country or area, by region	Type of survey	Country or area, by region	Type of survey
Africa		**Western Europe**	
Botswana	C	Austria	N
Egypt	C	Belgium	N
Lesotho	C	Denmark	N
Mozambique	C	Finland	N
Namibia	C	France	N
Nigeria	C	Germany	N
South Africa	C	Italy	N
Swaziland	C	Malta	N
Tunisia		Netherlands	N
Uganda	C	Norway	N
United Republic of Tanzania	C	Portugal	N
Zambia	C	Scotland	N
Zimbabwe	C	Spain	N and C
Asia		Sweden	N
Azerbaijan	C	Switzerland	N
Cambodia	C	United Kingdom	
China	C	England and Wales	N
India	C	Northern Ireland	N
Indonesia	C		
Japan	N	**Central and Eastern Europe**	
Kyrgyzstan	C	Albania	C
Mongolia	C	Belarus	C
Papua New Guinea	C	Bulgaria	C
Philippines	C	Croatia	C
Republic of Korea	C	Czech Republic	C
Latin America		Estonia	C
Argentina	C	Georgia	C
Bolivia	C	Hungary	C
Brazil	C	Latvia	C
Colombia	C	Lithuania	C
Costa Rica	C	Poland	N and C
Panama	C	Romania	C
Paraguay	C	Russian Federation	C
North America		Slovakia	C
Canada	N	Slovenia	
United States of America	N	The former Yugoslav Republic of Macedonia	C
Oceania		Ukraine	C
Australia	N	Yugoslavia	C
New Zealand	N		

The regional breakdown used in the Survey is intended to be an approximate grouping of countries that are geographically close to each other and that share some cultural values. However, countries within each region may differ significantly in terms of gross domestic product and their ranking on the United Nations Development Programme human development index (www.undp.org/currentHDR_E/).

Methodology

The Survey targets samples of households in which only one respondent, aged 16 or above, is selected. National samples include at least 2,000 respondents, who are generally interviewed using the computer-assisted telephone interview technique. In the countries where that method could not be used because of insufficient distribution of telephones, face-to-face interviews were conducted in the main cities, generally with samples of 1,000-1,500 respondents.

The questionnaire includes sections on 11 types of "conventional" crime, for which standard definitions are provided. Questions on consumer fraud and corruption are included; those are also accompanied by standard definitions. The questionnaire is also used to gather data on whether crimes were reported to the police, the reasons for not reporting crimes, attitudes towards the police, the fear of crime and crime prevention measures.

Of the eleven "conventional" crimes, some are "household crimes", that is, crimes that can be seen as affecting the household at large. Respondents report on all the incidents involving household crimes that are known to them. A first group of crimes deals with vehicles owned by the respondent or other members of his or her household: theft of car; theft from car; car vandalism; theft of bicycle; and theft of motorcycle. A second group refers to breaking and entering burglary; and attempted burglary. A third group of crimes refers to crimes experienced personally by the respondent: robbery; theft of personal property; assault or threat; and sexual incidents (women only). Finally, the questionnaire addresses two more types of crime that may have been experienced by the respondents: consumer fraud; and bribery or corruption.

Regular meetings of survey coordinators from participating countries have helped to facilitate the translation of concepts and definitions into the various languages.

Data analysis

Each sweep of the Survey provides an enormous amount of information. In-depth analysis of the database is one of the objectives of researchers across the world. The wealth of data produced can hardly be analysed between two consecutive sweeps of the Survey. Analysis of the Survey has been carried out mostly within comparable groups of countries, for example, national surveys in the "industrialized countries" city surveys in Central and Eastern Europe and the developing countries [2]. Analysis of the main comparative results concerning industrialized countries was published upon completion of the first, second, third and fourth international crime victim surveys [2-5]; results from developing countries and countries with economies in transition were made available in numerous publications [3-9]; and results from the International Crime Victim Survey 2000 were also widely published [10-13]. The present article will deal with some of the main findings of the Survey conducted in 2000. For international comparisons across groups, only respondents located in urban areas with populations of more than 100,000 are considered from national surveys.*

The crime count

The Survey provides an overall measure of victimization in the previous year through any of the 11 conventional crimes included in the questionnaire (which do not include consumer fraud and corruption). On average, approximately 28 per cent of respondents suffered at least one form of victimization over the twelve months preceding the interview. Overall victimization of around 27 per cent was observed in four out of six regions of the world (Western Europe, Central and Eastern Europe, North America and Australasia), while in Africa and Latin America much higher levels of victimization were observed (35 and 46 per cent respectively).

Figure I shows prevalence rates for burglary and robbery in the six world regions and Australia. In the Survey, burglary is defined as house-breaking for purposes of theft. It is a crime against the household that may involve very secure or poorly protected residences. While, in the industrialized world, burglars frequently steal objects of a very high value, such as jewellery or stereo equipment, burglary in developing countries is often aimed at stealing food, domestic appliances, linen or cutlery. In regions

---

*More information is available at the International Crime Victim Survey web site (www.unicri.it/icvs). It should be noted that, due to the increased number of participating countries, the groupings by region described in the present article differ from those discussed in earlier publications, such that direct comparisons with data presented elsewhere are not possible.

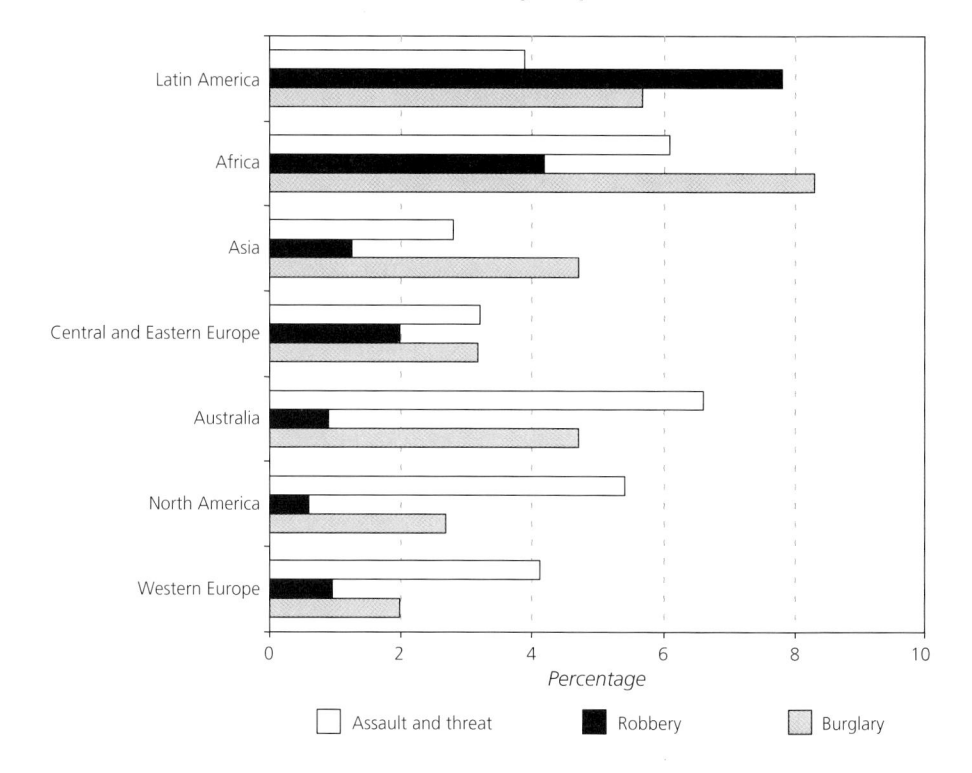

Figure I. Victimization rates for burglary, robbery, assault and threat, one-year period

where households have installed various levels of protection against burglary, such incidents tend to involve damage to doors, locks or windows. The Survey shows that this occurs more frequently in Western Europe, North America and Australia. Interestingly, the Survey shows that high levels of damage also occur in Africa during incidents of burglary.

The consequences of burglary in terms of monetary value may be very different in different contexts, although it is generally considered very serious, since it is a violation of the domestic sphere. It is therefore a crime that is well remembered by survey respondents and provides a reliable indicator of property crime.

Robbery is defined as theft from the person by use of force, thus involving direct contact between victim and offender (called "contact" crime). The crime category of assault and threat is defined in the Survey as personal aggression, by a stranger, relative or friend, without the purpose of stealing and is another contact crime. Although physical consequences in most cases may be minor, the crime may well have significant emotional repercussions for victims.

Figure I shows the regional distribution of victimization rates for burglaries, robberies and assaults and threats, as observed in the Survey. The differences among the regions were larger for the two crimes involving property of which the highest number occurred in Africa and Latin America. Burglary was over four times more frequent in Africa than in Western Europe. Robbery was approximately eight times higher in Latin America than in either Western Europe, North America or Australia. The data on robbery confirm the regional distribution of this crime as observed in official statistics on reported crime.

Rates of assault and threat showed smaller variations among regions: they were lowest in Central and Eastern Europe and Asia, and highest in Africa, North America and Australia.

Previous analysis using the Survey data at the aggregate level showed a negative correlation between the human development index and property crime [7]. The 2000 Survey data confirmed that levels and effects of victimization are more pronounced in the developing countries than in the rest of the world. That contrasts sharply with the fact that official recorded crime levels in developed countries are far higher than in developing countries [1].

Crimes reported to the police

Crimes are more frequently reported to the police in Western Europe, North America and Australia than in the other regions, thus showing an opposite trend with respect to the frequency of victimization. It is concluded that in the regions where more crime occurs, the police know less about it.

In general, car theft was the most frequently reported crime, followed by burglary (see figure II). However, the considerable differences that exist among countries and regions in respect of insurance coverage (since a valid report to the police is a requirement in order to submit a claim to an insurance company, it is expected that reporting is more frequent in the areas where house insurance is more common) and the ease of reporting (determined by factors such as access to the police, availability of telephones, and so forth) result in different reporting patterns. Burglary was more frequently reported in Western Europe, North America and Australia.

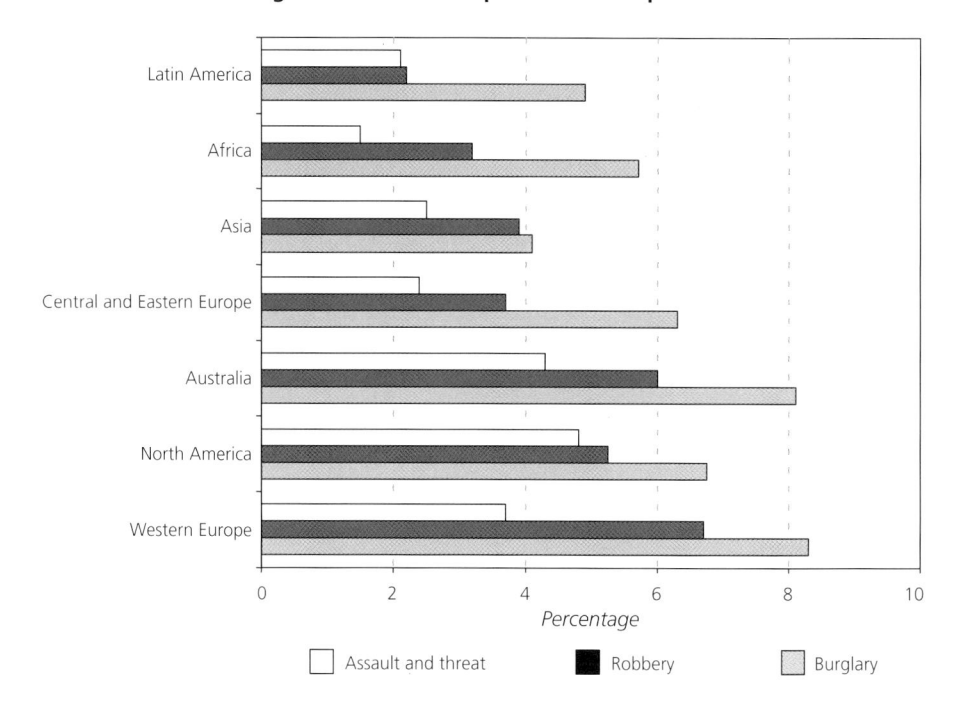

Figure II. Crimes reported to the police

[Bar chart showing percentages of assault and threat, robbery, and burglary reported to police by region: Latin America, Africa, Asia, Central and Eastern Europe, Australia, North America, Western Europe]

Robbery was also frequently reported in Western Europe, but much less in the other studied regions, in particular in Latin America, where only one victim of robbery out of five reported to the police. Again, this is consistent with the conclusions reached by Shaw, van Dijk and Rhomberg [1]. It appears that the greater the level of crime, the smaller the number of citizens willing to approach the police. More than 50 per cent of the Latin American victims of robbery who did not report the crime to the police said they did so because "the police would not do anything" and approximately 25 per cent of them said that they feared or disliked the police.

Assault and threat was the least frequently reported crime, with rates around or below 40 per cent in all regions. Significantly, levels of reporting did not show any variations since the previous analysis of the 1996 Survey results.

Trends in victimization, 1996-2000

An analysis of regional trends can be made by comparing victimization rates in the countries that took part in both the 1996 and 2000 sweeps of the Survey.* The comparison reveals that victimization rates are consistent in most regions and modest variations have been registered, with an overall trend downwards for the three types of crime considered.**

The biggest changes, both upwards and downwards, were found in Latin America and Africa, where rates of robbery increased considerably (contrary to what was observed in the other regions) and burglary decreased more sharply than in the other regions (see figure III). This conclusion is again consistent with the analysis of Shaw, van Dijk and Rhomberg [1].

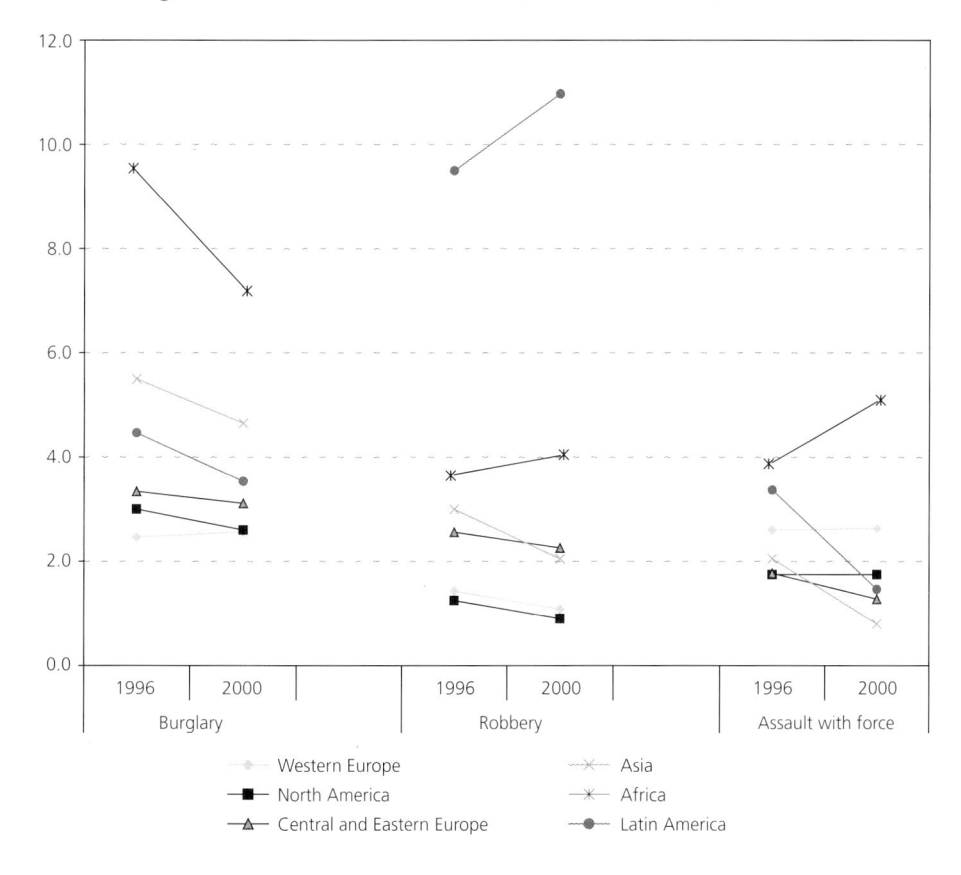

Figure III. Trends in victimization, selected crimes, 1996-2000

---

*The analysis of trends at the regional level only included the 31 countries that participated in the International Crime Victim Survey in 1996 and 2000. Fewer countries are therefore included in each region and they are not the same countries as those presented in the analysis of the 2000 Survey. Possible inconsistencies in sampling procedure suggest that some caution should be exercised in reading trends, especially as regards developing countries.

**This section deals with data on burglary, robbery and assault with force, that is, only the portion of incidents in the assault and threat category that involved the use of force.

As regards assault with force, aside from the relatively steady trend observed in Western Europe and North America and a slight decrease in Central and Eastern Europe, developing countries show large variations that do not allow for easy interpretation. While Asia and Latin America showed a downward trend, assaults increased in Africa.

Corruption and consumer fraud

Questions on the direct experience of respondents with corruption or bribery of public officials are one of the unique features of the Survey.* Due to the scarcity of available information, corruption is often measured by surveys. The International Crime Victim Survey offers the advantage of addressing citizens with questions on corruption from the point of view of crime and victimization, thus highlighting that having to pay a bribe is a form of abuse of power that entails being victimized. Such an approach facilitates understanding of the question across cultures and partially lifts the burden from the respondent to admit that he or she also did something wrong by agreeing to pay. International Crime Victim Survey data have been extensively used for assessing corruption in several areas, if not as an absolute measure of the phenomenon, at least to compare with other available indicators [14-15].

There is a high level of consistency between 1996 and 2000 results from the Survey, with a slight decrease in victimization rates for both corruption and consumer fraud. As regards regional comparisons, it should be noted that corruption in Western Europe, North America and Australia is almost non-existent, while it is a widespread phenomenon in the rest of the world.

The analysis of the type of public official who most frequently demanded bribes revealed the extensive involvement of police officers in corruption. This is a critical issue in the complicated relationship between the police and the community that is also reflected in the overall assessment of police performance.

Consumer fraud of some sort, especially when dealing with retail stores, was experienced by some 9 per cent of respondents in Western Europe and in North America and Australia. Victimization rates for such fraud were much higher in the other regions and especially in Central and Eastern European countries (see figure IV).

---

*The question on corruption was as follows: "In some areas there is a problem of corruption among government or public officials. During 1999, has any government official, for instance a customs officer, police officer or inspector, in your own country asked you or expected you to pay a bribe for his service?"

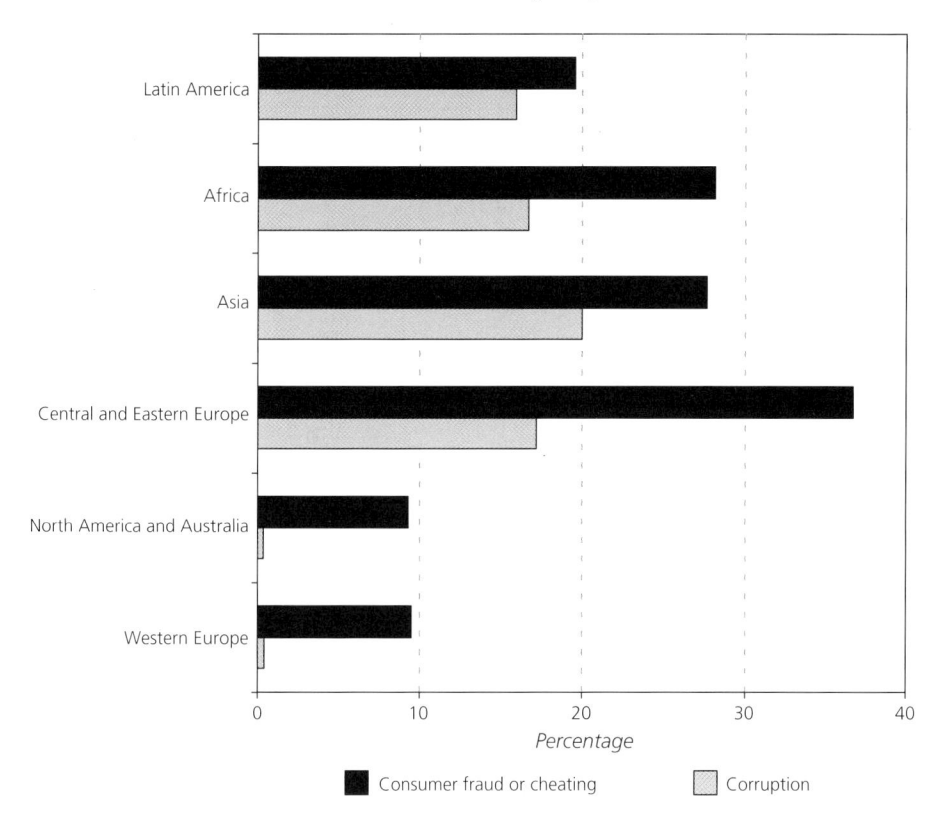

Figure IV. Victimization rates for corruption and consumer fraud, one-year period

[Bar chart showing victimization rates by region for Consumer fraud or cheating and Corruption, percentages from 0 to 40]

Assessment of police performance

The section of the Survey dealing with the assessment of police performance (figure V) revealed that respondents in Latin America, Central and Eastern Europe and Africa had low levels of satisfaction with police efforts in preventing and controlling crime.* This suggests that in many countries there is still much to be done by police services in order to gain public confidence.

Because of a change in the 2000 questionnaire, it is not possible to analyse directly trends in public opinion of police performance. It appears, however,

---

*The question on satisfaction with the police in controlling crime was as follows: "Taking everything into account, how good do you think the police in your area are at controlling crime? Do you think they do a very good job, a fairly good job, a fairly poor job or a very poor job?" Figure V shows percentages for the answers "very good" and "fairly good".

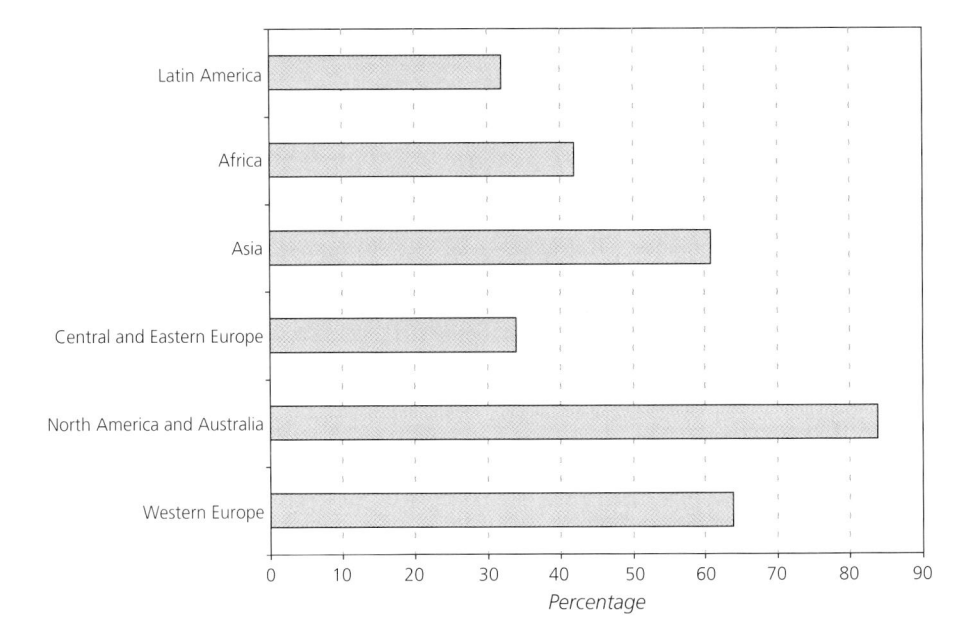

Figure V. Satisfaction with the police in controlling crime

Region	Percentage
Latin America	~32
Africa	~42
Asia	~60
Central and Eastern Europe	~33
North America and Australia	~84
Western Europe	~63

that respondents tended to express their opinion of the police more freely than in previous sweeps of the Survey. Indeed, the percentage of respondents falling in the "don't know" category was very small.

A correlation was observed between satisfaction with the police and reporting to the police for the various types of crime. The correlation is stronger for reporting assault and threat, which is the least reported type of crime (r 0.473, N = 47). It appears, therefore, that a good perception of the police may increase public cooperation with that service.

Conclusion

By disclosing previously unrevealed aspects of crime and victimization at the international level, the International Crime Victim Survey has become an indispensable source of information for researchers, policy makers and the international community. In particular, inclusion in indexes (such as the Transparency International Corruption Perceptions Index (www.transparency.org/cpi/index.html#cpi) and global reports (such as the *Human Development Report* (www.undp.org/currentHDR_E/), the *Global Report on Crime and Justice* [16], the *World Report on Violence and Health* [17], the *European Sourcebook of Crime and Criminal Justice Statistics* [18], the *Global*

Corruption Report [14] and *Crime and Criminal Justice in Europe and North America, 1990-1994*) [19]. The International Crime Victim Survey has also been included in the United Nations *Manual for the Development of a System of Criminal Justice Statistics* [20].

It is expected that, in the future, the International Crime Victim Survey will become an even more solid source of data, because a greater number of countries will be included and those which have already participated will continue to do so, thus reinforcing the longitudinal series. An effort in the direction of further standardization of data collection is currently being made by the group coordinating the project [21]. The involvement of institutional partners such as the Justice Department of Canada, the Ministry of Justice of the Netherlands and the Home Office of the United Kingdom of Great Britain and Northern Ireland, together with the United Nations Office on Drugs and Crime and the United Nations Interregional Crime and Justice Research Institute ensures the monitoring and coordination of activities at the central level. It is also expected that, in future, the International Crime against Business Survey and the International Violence against Women Survey, which are currently under development, will play important roles in complementing the International Crime Victim Survey in the areas of crime against businesses and violence against women.

References

1. Mark Shaw, Jan van Dijk and Wolfgang Rhomberg, "Determining trends in global crime and justice", *Forum on Crime and Society*, vol. 3, Nos. 1-2 (2003).
2. J. J. M. van Dijk, P. Mayhew and M. Killias, *Experiences of Crime across the World: Key Findings from the 1989 International Crime Survey* (Deventer, Kluwer Law and Taxation, 1990).
3. A. Alvazzi del Frate, U. Zvekic and J. J. M. van Dijk, eds., *Understanding Crime: Experiences of Crime and Crime Control*, UNICRI publication No. 57 (Rome, United Nations Interregional Crime and Justice Research Institute, 1993).
4. P. Mayhew and J. J. M. van Dijk, *Criminal Victimisation in Eleven Industrialised Countries: Key Findings from the 1996 International Crime Victims Survey*, No. 162 (The Hague, Netherlands, Ministry of Justice, 1997).
5. J. van Kesteren, P. Mayhew and P. Nieuwbeerta, *Criminal Victimisation in Seventeen Industrialised Countries: Key Findings from the 2000 International Crime Victims Survey*, No. 187 (The Hague, Netherlands, Ministry of Justice, 2000).
6. U. Zvekic and A. Alvazzi del Frate, eds., *Criminal Victimisation in the Developing World*, UNICRI publication No. 55 (Rome, United Nations Interregional Crime and Justice Research Institute, 1995).

7. A. Alvazzi del Frate, *Victims of Crime in the Developing World*, UNICRI publication No. 57 (Rome, United Nations Interregional Crime and Justice Research Institute, 1998).

8. O. Hatalak, A. Alvazzi del Frate and U. Zvekic, eds., *The International Crime Victim Survey in Countries in Transition: National Reports*, UNICRI publication No. 62 (Rome, United Nations Interregional Crime and Justice Research Institute, 2000).

9. U. Zvekic, *Criminal Victimisation in Countries in Transition*, UNICRI publication No. 61 (Rome, United Nations Interregional Crime and Justice Research Institute, 1998).

10. A. Alvazzi del Frate, "Criminal victimisation in Latin America", *Crime Victimization in Comparative Perspective*, P. Nieuwbeerta, ed. (The Hague, Netherlands, Boom Juridische Uitgevers, 2002).

11. A. Alvazzi del Frate and J. van Kesteren, "Criminal victimization in Eastern-Central Europe", *Crime Victimization in Comparative Perspective*, P. Nieuwbeerta, ed. (The Hague, Netherlands, Boom Juridische Uitgevers, 2002).

12. A. Alvazzi del Frate and J. van Kesteren, "The ICVS in the developing world", *International Journal of Comparative Criminology*, vol. 2, No. 1 (2003).

13. B. Naudé and J. Prinsloo, "Crime victimization in Southern Africa", *Crime Victimization in Comparative Perspective*, P. Nieuwbeerta, ed. (The Hague, Netherlands, Boom Juridische Uitgevers, 2002).

14. Transparency International, *Global Corruption Report 2001*, R. Hoddess, J. Bonfield and T. Wolfe, eds. (Berlin, 2001).

15. U. Zvekic and L. Camerer, "Corruption in Southern Africa: a surveys-based overview", *Corruption and Anti-Corruption in Southern Africa*, U. Zvekic, ed. (United Nations Office on Drugs and Crime, Regional Office for Southern Africa, 2002).

16. United Nations, Office for Drug Control and Crime Prevention, *Global Report on Crime and Justice* (New York, Oxford University Press, 1999).

17. World Health Organization, *World Report on Violence and Health* (Geneva, 2002). Available at www.who.int/violence_injury_prevention/violence/world_report/wrvh1/en/.

18. Council of Europe, *European Sourcebook of Crime and Criminal Justice Statistics* (Strasbourg, Council of Europe, 1999). Available at www.europeansourcebook.org/esb/index.html.

19. K. Kangaspunta, M. Joutsen and N. Ollus, eds., *Crime and Criminal Justice in Europe and North America, 1990-1994* (Helsinki, European Institute for Crime Prevention and Control, affiliated with the United Nations, 1998).

20. *Manual for the Development of a System of Criminal Justice Statistics* (United Nations publication, Sales No. E.03.XVII.6).

21. A. Alvazzi del Frate, "The future of the International Crime Victim Survey", *International Journal of Comparative Criminology*, vol. 2, No. 1 (2003).

MEASURING AND TAKING ACTION AGAINST CRIME IN SOUTHERN AFRICA

by Rob Boone,* Gary Lewis** and Ugljesa Zvekic***

Abstract

The 11 member States of the Southern African Development Community (SADC), despite the diversity of their populations and political, economic and social systems, share many of the same problems, including one of the highest levels of organized crime in the world. The present article gives an overview of the crime situation and trends in the SADC member States, despite the poor collation capacity and therefore the scarcity of data. The article highlights that these problems are much more a developmental concern than a law enforcement matter. The article outlines the situation in the region in terms of criminal justice and crime policies. It also lists some drug and crime priorities, arising from the experience of the United Nations Office on Drugs and Crime in the region in the past three years in order to promote effective and long-term changes.

Regional overview: general characteristics****

The 11 countries that are the subject of the analysis offered in the present article (Angola, Botswana, Democratic Republic of the Congo, Lesotho, Malawi, Mozambique, Namibia, South Africa, Swaziland, Zambia and

---

*Representative, Southern Africa, United Nations Office on Drugs and Crime, Regional Office for Southern Africa.

**Representative, United Nations Office on Drugs and Crime, India. Formerly Programme Manager (Drugs), United Nations Office on Drugs and Crime, Regional Office for Southern Africa.

***Senior Crime Prevention and Criminal Justice Expert, United Nations Office on Drugs and Crime, Regional Office for Southern Africa.

****Prompted by the need to explore the various types and the magnitude of drug and crime issues and the responses to them, and with a mandate from its headquarters, the Regional Office for Southern Africa of the United Nations Office on Drugs and Crime, based in Pretoria, devised and sponsored a conference to develop a regional strategic programme framework on drugs and crime. The conference, which was organized in Benoni, South Africa on 5 to 7 August 2002, for all SADC member States, designed to provide an ideal opportunity to collect and analyse information and to provide a systematic means of developing a programme of training and technical assistance projects. The main objective of the conference was to identify points of convergence of priority areas for action by the regional stakeholders in drug control, crime prevention and criminal justice reform. On the basis of the materials collected for and at the conference, as well as reports from missions throughout the region, professional articles and experience gained over the past several years, the Regional Office has prepared a draft strategic programme framework on drugs and crime for Southern Africa. The present article, which focuses mainly on crime is based on that document.

Zimbabwe)* display an enormous diversity of population, political systems and levels of economic and social development. Despite this variety, they share many common features, including formidable problems of poverty, underdevelopment, the human immunodeficiency virus/acquired immunodeficiency syndrome (HIV/AIDS) pandemic, massive food shortages, social inequities, vast economic inequalities and, in some countries, political instability and conflicts.** Such are the circumstances that foster some of the highest crime levels in the world. The growth of organized crime, which is often connected with drug trafficking, is intensifying the already difficult tasks of prevention, enforcement and prosecution.

While the region faces immense socio-economic and institutional challenges, the present article evaluates the situation against a series of positive factors. With the advent of democracy in South Africa in 1994, the most powerful State in the region has been able to turn its attention and energies to the task of advancing the economic empowerment of all its citizens and promoting a similar empowerment among its neighbours. SADC holds the promise of fruitful regional cooperation in its institutional framework, which is currently being reorganized. All the SADC member States are also members of the African Union and, to varying degrees, are likely to participate in the New Partnership for Africa's Development (NEPAD), which was endorsed by the African Union in July 2002 and which itself has the potential to promote integration and socio-economic advancement in the region.

SADC has established a number of institutions and organizations whose effective functioning is vital to the fight against crime and drugs in the region. These bodies are in both the public sector and within civil society. The non-governmental organizations in the region have received limited attention, yet they are a vital component. The work of both local and international non-governmental organizations is, for example, indispensable

---

*The area of responsibility of the Regional Office for Southern Africa extends to 11 of the 14 SADC member States. Therefore, while all SADC member States were involved in the strategic programme framework exercise to a certain degree, and certainly the regional drug and crime problems do not stop at the borders of the countries covered by the Regional Office, the present article covers only 11 of those States. The other three SADC member States, Mauritius, Seychelles and the United Republic of Tanzania, fall under the responsibility of the Regional Office for Eastern Africa, based in Nairobi.

**According to the Human Development Index for 2002, prepared by the United Nations Development Programme, Angola, the Democratic Republic of the Congo, Malawi, Mozambique and Zambia are categorized as countries experiencing "low human development", while the other six countries of the present analysis fall into the lowest part of the "medium human development" category, with the exception of South Africa, which nevertheless falls into the lower part of the "medium human development" category.

in anti-corruption campaigns. At the same time, such non-governmental organizations are extremely vulnerable owing to funding problems and, in some cases, to harassment from both state officials and organized criminal groups. For instance, since 1994 South African non-governmental organizations have suffered as international donors have tended to switch their assistance from civil society entities to Government-to-Government projects. That trend is now reversing somewhat as shown by the degree of cooperation with the quasi-state organization, the SADC Epidemiological Network on Drug Abuse (SENDU), and a range of other civil society entities.

SADC has established a Drug Control Committee and the Southern African Forum against Corruption was founded in 1999. Efforts are under way to establish an anti-corruption civil society network in the region. The International Law Enforcement Academy in Gaborone is another important institution in this field.

The key law enforcement association in the region is the Southern African Regional Police Chiefs Co-operation Organisation (SARPCCO), which is operationally headed by national police commissioners. Its governing body is comprised of the respective ministers to whom the commissioners report. It is closely involved with the work of SADC on crime prevention and drug abuse and has also operated with some success in coordinating police efforts against transnational crime. The work of the Sub-regional Bureau for Southern Africa of the International Criminal Police Organization (Interpol) in Harare is also of relevance, including in its role as the SARPCCO secretariat. Both these organizations can draw on significant resources at the regional and international levels.

All these regional bodies need financial and technical assistance and strong political support to carry out their mandates effectively. Continued support in this regard and encouragement for reform among law enforcement, judicial and correctional agencies in the region as a whole, remain key priorities for the United Nations Office on Drugs and Crime in liaison with other bodies. The specifics of the crime and drug situation of Southern Africa are reviewed against this background.

Overview of the regional crime situation

As would be expected in a region as large and diverse as that of SADC, a regional summary of crime trends involves generalizations that do not necessarily hold true for each individual member State. Nevertheless, the following broad statements seem warranted:

  (a) Key officials and informed observers throughout the region believe that criminal activities, coupled, in the case of organized crime, with drug trafficking, pose a heightened threat to effective governance and to improving the social fabric;

  (b) The extent of this threat varies from country to country and in several cases is an element of a broader problem, such as ongoing civil strife or political fragmentation. One cause for optimism is that current political negotiations in the most severely affected countries may, in the medium term, bring about greater political stability in the region as a whole;

  (c) Official capacity for data collection and analysis of crime and drug patterns is generally poor and is unevenly distributed. In several countries this capacity barely exists. Effective law enforcement, criminal justice and drug control strategies are considerably less feasible where basic information is lacking. There is also a scarcity of information based on victim surveys. In general, the dearth of drug, crime and criminal justice information seriously impedes the formulation, evaluation and analysis of operational programmes, as well as of training and assistance programmes designed to facilitate them;

  (d) Under-resourced and inexperienced officials in key agencies struggle to assimilate the international assistance that is available. This problem is compounded by the often slow and incomplete implementation of the training and technical assistance programmes themselves;

  (e) The consensus, in particular among law enforcement and criminal justice agencies of the region, appears to be that the drug issue is a subset of the larger crime and social disintegration problems, except to the extent that drug abuse is an issue in terms of health and welfare;

  (f) If crime prevention capacities are generally weak, there is little hope that a focus on fighting drug trafficking and substance abuse can forge ahead without strengthening the broader crime prevention and law enforcement mechanisms. Thus, what is needed is a broad strategy to promote prevention, enhance the rule of law, strengthen law enforcement and judicial integrity and foster treatment and rehabilitation, so that energies can be brought to bear on the most acute problem areas, including drugs;

  (g) Arguably there is a case for viewing certain aspects of the drug problem, notably specific rises in the consumption of drugs, as organic outgrowths of social disintegration and the increased availability of drugs. In such circumstances, the causal link between crime and drugs is less direct or may even be reversed.

Crime trends

Several SADC member States have virtually no capacity to gather or collate crime data and only a few have carried out victim surveys.* Noting these limitations in terms of information, the observations presented below regarding trends in the major crime categories must be treated with caution.

Serious and violent crime is a problem throughout the region. The incidence of such crime appears to be particularly acute in South Africa. The most recent report of the United Nations Office on Drugs and Crime, from November 2002, "South Africa: country profile on drugs and crime", highlights that violent crime has shown a general increase since 1994, with a slight downturn in the period 2001-2002. However, these recorded rates, which parallel the highest rates from other parts of the world, may in part be explained, on the one hand, by a greater propensity to report crimes to the police and, on the other hand, by a relatively efficient data collection capacity compared with other countries in the region and elsewhere.

Undoubtedly, firearms, both legal and illegal, are used in a significant percentage of the serious and violent crimes committed in the region and in the various activities of organized criminals. There is a lack of data in this regard and a great deal of research is needed. That said, in 2002 SADC adopted a Protocol on the Control of Firearms, Ammunition and Other Related Materials, although none of the SADC member States has signed

---

*There were no relevant statistics provided at all in the case of Angola and the Democratic Republic of the Congo. Zambia has not provided crime data from the police, though court records from the period 1998-1999 act as a partial substitute. Mozambique has provided some aggregated data for the period 1998-2001. Lesotho and Namibia have little or no crime data from the police covering the last three years, though earlier figures give some idea of trends. Official data for Botswana and Zimbabwe appear to be available only up to 2000, although before that year the statistics are useful. Swaziland's statistics are available in some cases up to 2001, but they are fragmentary. Similarly, Malawi has provided some crime data up to 2001. Only South Africa provides relatively detailed and up-to-date official crime data from the police reporting network. Even here, problems with the collection methodology and analysis led the Government of South Africa to place a moratorium on the release of crime statistics from the police for the year 2001. However, the recently released annual report of the South African police service for 2001/2002 establishes a certain level of consistency for crime trends over a period of eight years (1994-2002). Other criminal justice statistics, such as prosecutorial, court and prison data, are even less available across the region. Since the mid-1990s, the United Nations Interregional Crime and Justice Research Institute, in cooperation with the African Institute for the Prevention of Crime and the Treatment of Offenders, and the Department of Criminology of the University of South Africa, has carried out the International Crime Victim Survey in the capital and/or largest cities of Botswana, Lesotho, Namibia, South Africa, Swaziland, Zambia and Zimbabwe, as well as in three selected urban areas in Mozambique. Despite certain limitations in the Survey in Southern Africa, it represents an important source of information on crime and criminal justice performance in the region. Among the SADC member States, apparently the only national victim survey was carried out in South Africa in 1998 (with the assistance of the United Nations).

the Protocol against the Illicit Manufacturing of and Trafficking in Firearms, Their Parts and Components and Ammunition, supplementing the United Nations Convention against Transnational Organized Crime (General Assembly resolution 55/255, annex).

Within the region, Botswana appears to have the lowest homicide rate, although assault cases have climbed quite steeply in recent years. Namibia may rank next lowest in homicide, although the latest data are from 1998.

Property-related crimes, as elsewhere, appear to comprise the bulk of reported cases in those countries with any data. High rates of car theft and cross-border smuggling of vehicles, especially from South Africa, constitute a major police problem. Some theft is relatively specific to the region. For example, livestock theft is widely reported even in the urban areas covered by the International Crime Victim Survey studies.

The many types of property crime and the various ways they are classified by the police make comparisons among countries and over time complicated and in some cases unreliable. However, one form of property crime, burglary, is perhaps worth singling out. It is one of the most personally intrusive and feared crimes that stops short of actual violence. It is also one crime on which data from the end of the 1990s are available from victimization surveys in several SADC member States (see table). Burglary, or housebreaking with entry (as opposed to attempted burglary), represents a risk to most citizens because most people have a residence.

Burglary victimization rates in main urban areas, selected countries in Southern Africa

Country	Urban area	Period	Victimization rate (percentage of respondents)
Botswana	. .		6.6
Lesotho	Maseru	1998	4.1
Mozambique	Three unnamed urban areas	2002	13.4
Namibia	Windhoek	1999	8.0
South Africa	Johannesburg	1999	8.0 (7.2)[a]
Swaziland	Mbabane and Manzini	1998	9.0
Zambia	Lusaka	1999	10.9
Zimbabwe	Harare	1996-1997	7.2

Source: International Crime Victim Survey.

[a] Victimization rate at the national level, based on data from the South African National Victims of Crime Survey conducted in 1998, is shown in parentheses.

Crimes related to violence against women, especially but not only rape, constitute a disturbing phenomenon that appears to be endemic in the region. All countries for which some figures are available from police or survey sources report high and, for the most part, increasing rates of such violence. Once again, the situation appears to be at its worst in South Africa, where the reported rate of rape is at the highest level in the world; however, an increased incidence of rape has also been reported in Botswana, Lesotho, Namibia and Zimbabwe.

Organized crime appears to be on the increase in much, if not all, of the region, although it is a relatively new phenomenon. Many groups engaged in so-called "organized crime" are merely small, loose and shifting groups of no more than 5-10 individuals who plan armed robberies and bank heists. Reports of such groupings are found in communications of the police services in Botswana, Namibia, Swaziland and Zimbabwe. Organized crime as a criminological phenomenon, however, covers a wide spectrum of organizational types [1]. Often complicit in high-level official corruption, more extensive and enduring criminal networks in the region appear to be behind the rise in laundering of illicit drug proceeds and such networks help drive the trafficking in firearms, stolen vehicles and endangered species.

Owing to its special geopolitical position and economic opportunities, South Africa is used as the regional hub for organized crime, including drug trafficking. The increase in organized criminal activities in South Africa has been accentuated since 1994 by the ending of its international isolation, its much freer and more extensive international trade and commerce, and its well-developed financial, communication and transportation systems. According to the South African Police Service, that there are more than 230 criminal "syndicates" operating both within and across the country's borders [2]. Some organized criminal rings concentrate on specific activities, such as those run by various drug lords who dominate the illicit importation and distribution of cocaine and heroin in South Africa (and who are said to be nationals of Nigeria but, in some cases, are actually nationals of other West African countries).

All drug control efforts are likely to face organized opposition and such efforts must become increasingly sophisticated to counter the expertise of drug syndicates that are simultaneously engaged in other criminal activities. Much work is under way in terms of promulgating legislation against organized crime, particularly in view of the requirements of the United Nations Convention against Transnational Organized Crime (General Assembly resolution 55/25, annex I). With the exception of the Democratic Republic of the Congo, the United Republic of Tanzania and Zambia, all

SADC member States have signed the Convention and Namibia and Botswana have ratified it. There remain several key challenges for ratification and implementation of the Convention. These challenges relate to (a) the weakness of the economic and financial systems as they pertain to money-laundering; (b) domestic legislation for the four mandatory offences under the Convention, namely, participation in organized criminal activity, money-laundering, corruption and obstruction of justice; and (c) harmonization of laws regarding extradition, mutual legal assistance and confiscation and forfeiture of proceeds of crime [3]. It is expected that the draft SADC protocols on extradition and on mutual legal assistance in criminal matters will greatly facilitate the harmonization of domestic legislation to meet the requirements of the Convention.

Efforts are under way to establish law enforcement units to counter organized crime, but the majority of the SADC member States do not have such integrated units. Instead, they generally have units that specialize in, for example, vehicle theft, serious crime and crime involving gold and diamonds. South Africa is exemplary in terms of the units to counter organized crime both within the police and within the prosecution service.

Corruption, like organized crime, is an omnibus term referring to a host of activities. It encompasses bribes to police, customs and judicial officers, teachers, medical personnel and other state officials in exchange for special favours or for services rendered that the bribed official was otherwise obligated to provide. Corruption can also refer to criminal activity that may undermine the foundations of political, financial and administrative integrity at the highest levels and it can involve illegal transactions worth millions if not billions of dollars.

According to an analysis of the results of a regional seminar on anticorruption investigating strategies for SADC member States [4], corruption is increasingly perceived as a serious problem in the region, although, from an international perspective, the SADC region fares much better than Africa as a whole. In a survey conducted in the region, business leaders were considered corrupt by more than half of those responding. The public sector was seen as disproportionately more vulnerable to corruption than the private sector and corruption was considered to be centred in law enforcement and the delivery of basic services. Corruption in varying degrees is perceived as quite widespread in all SADC member States, but appears to be of particular concern in countries that are undergoing or have undergone the devastation of civil war (Angola, the Democratic Republic of the Congo and Mozambique).

Findings of research carried out at the regional level show that there is a huge gap between perceived levels of corruption and actual experience with corruption and that citizens on average feel that their Governments are not sufficiently committed to combating corruption [4]. It should be noted, however, that in almost all the countries in the region a great deal of legislative anti-corruption work is taking place, in particular in view of the recently adopted and signed SADC Protocol against Corruption. Similarly, half of the SADC member States have established dedicated anti-corruption agencies and another five members are contemplating the establishment of such agencies. These agencies operate with different degrees of effectiveness and independence, as the extent of political support given to them varies [4]. The dual phenomenon of trafficking in persons and smuggling of migrants exists in the region. Regional trafficking in persons comprises trafficking in women and children both from Asia and Eastern Europe into the region and from the region into Europe, North America and Asia. It also includes intraregional trafficking and in-country trafficking, particularly trafficking in children. The smuggling of migrants, in particular the smuggling of migrants from countries devastated by political and social unrest and poverty, including famine, appears to be a huge problem in the region. South Africa is used as a hub, both as a destination and as a transit country, while Mozambique and Swaziland are known transit points. Much of the intraregional trafficking is southwards to the wealthier southern tier of the region. Groups engaged in transnational organized crime (both locally based groups and others) are heavily involved in trafficking in humans and smuggling of migrants, but much more systematic research needs to be conducted on the magnitude of these two crimes and on the exploitation of the victims. Throughout the region, there is an absolute lack of legislation and law enforcement capacity to deal with these problems. Although a majority of SADC member States have signed the United Nations Convention against Transnational Organized Crime, not all that signed the Convention have signed the two Protocols supplementing the Convention on these matters: the Protocol to Prevent, Suppress and Punish Trafficking in Persons, Especially Women and Children (General Assembly resolution 55/25, annex II) and the Protocol against the Smuggling of Migrants by Land, Sea and Air (General Assembly resolution 55/25, annex III). Botswana and Namibia have ratified all three instruments. In addition, at least four countries in the region have reported a problem of trafficking in human body parts.

The new patterns of organized crime, drug trafficking and terrorist financing, centred on South Africa, with its relative wealth and sophisticated economy and financial sector, have placed the issue of money-laundering firmly on the agenda of a number of key SADC member States.

The laundering of drug proceeds through the international banking system is rendered easier by inadequate preparation and countermeasures on the part of States only recently exposed to the activities of criminal cartels. The situation seems particularly critical in the short term for Lesotho, Mozambique, Namibia and Swaziland, which are neighbours of the commercial and financial magnet of South Africa, as well as in that country itself. Drug money, for example, is reported to be moving into property and construction in Mozambique and the case may well be similar in South Africa. A total of 9 of the 11 countries covered in the present article, all except Angola and the Democratic Republic of the Congo, are eligible to participate in the recently inaugurated 14-member Eastern and Southern Africa Anti-Money Laundering Group, which has its secretariat in Dar es Salaam.

Criminal justice

Regarding police performance, 66 per cent of respondents to the International Crime Victim Survey in Botswana reported being satisfied with overall police performance in controlling crime; the figures were 53 per cent, 52 per cent and 46 per cent for Mozambique, Zambia and South Africa, respectively. By contrast, however, the same survey shows high levels of public dissatisfaction with the way police handle crimes actually reported, ranging from dissatisfaction by 69.3 per cent of respondents in Zambia, 55.7 per cent in South Africa, 49.9 per cent in Botswana and 47.5 per cent in Namibia to less than one third in Swaziland and Lesotho. As for sub-Saharan police forces as a whole, independent analysis casts doubt on the degree of attention given to the civil and political rights of citizens, adding that police officials are generally poorly paid [5]. While some of the SADC member States in the southern tier may be a partial exception to this general statement, policing capacity is clearly one of the key governance challenges facing most of these States.

Data suggest that prisons suffer from gross overcrowding, with a figure of 100 per cent in the case of Botswana [6] and 68 per cent in South Africa. Courts of the region have also been found in the main to lack resources, to have a large backlog of criminal cases and to lack trained legal personnel. They are also physically inaccessible to large portions of the population [7].

Policies

In principle, all SADC member States have shown their willingness to align their crime and drug policies with the major international instruments or to formulate regional protocols that incorporate current global thinking, including resolutions and guidelines of United Nations bodies. On crime and drug policies, there are no maverick States in the region, nor are there powerful constituencies attempting to challenge the dominant international paradigm. Little local support appears to exist, for example, to decriminalize cannabis use.

Where States in the region have been hesitant to commit to international agreements and best practices, the major reason appears to be that the Governments lack either the capacity or the political will to implement specific obligations under a convention or agreement to change their legal and governance systems.

A total of 7 of the 11 SADC member States reviewed in the present article have developed, or are developing, crime prevention and control strategies, with South Africa the most notable example, as shown by the 2000-2002 National Crime Combating Strategy of the South African Police Service. However, crime prevention strategies in the region have not advanced as far as drug control strategies.

SADC member States have made some progress towards regional agreements and operational cooperation in crime and drug control. Although, at the country level, the overall picture may be marked by ad hoc plans and projects, it is clear that the SADC member States are willing and able to cooperate with considerable success in a number of areas. One example is the completion of several successes, under "Operation Rachel", a joint project in Mozambique and South Africa for the destruction of small arms. Similarly, the projects funded by the United Nations Office on Drugs and Crime on drug interdiction at both seaports and land border posts in Mozambique, South Africa and Swaziland have had some major seizures to their credit.

SARPCCO, which includes all the countries covered in the present article with the exception of the Democratic Republic of the Congo, has ensured that the SADC member States are conscious of the growing problem of cross-border organized crime and has promoted active steps to combat it.*

---

*For instance, in response to the questionnaire sent out in preparation for the workshop on crime information and organized crime threat analysis, organized jointly by the United Nations Office on Drugs and Crime and SARPCCO in South Africa in April 2002, the responding police agencies stated that progress was being made in fighting organized vehicle theft by the introduction of a regional vehicle clearance certificate system. In general, the respondents indicated that the region's police agencies were keen for much more regional cooperation, inter alia, through far more sharing of information on organized criminal networks and methods to combat them.

Priorities

When looking at social capital from a long-term perspective, the need to overcome endemic criminal activity and trafficking in and consumption of drugs in Southern Africa is much more a developmental concern than a law enforcement matter. Economic growth, healthier and more highly educated populations and the strengthening of major institutions such as the civil service are likely to generate both the will and the capacity to act more decisively on this front. However, in the short and medium terms, much can be done by judiciously targeted interventions that countermand serious criminality and the associated drug trafficking. There is also scope for effective prevention, treatment and rehabilitation activities in the areas of both crime and drug control.

Various projects in recent years, usually undertaken with international donor assistance, have begun to make a positive difference in a variety of areas, ranging from border control and cross-border law enforcement initiatives to the upgrading of police and judicial capacities. These have been accomplished by significant training, research and technical assistance projects. Initiatives have also begun, albeit more recently, in the fields of prevention, treatment and rehabilitation.

Of course, both the challenges of this troubled region and the resources required to meet them are immense. Properly, international donors will continue to look for a measurable impact from their interventions. What is required now is a clear set of priorities with assistance efforts focused around them. Such efforts should draw on the lessons of the past and the outcome of evidence-based analysis.

One lesson suggests that for all priority assistance areas, but especially for those of prevention, enforcement, treatment and rehabilitation, civil society organizations have a vital role to play. For example, numerous initiatives throughout the region involve non-governmental organizations that actively uncover corruption and support rehabilitation and awareness-raising campaigns, while others promote human rights among police forces. Recent years have also witnessed the growth of grass-roots community organizations performing invaluable work at the local level. Many such initiatives support HIV/AIDS awareness and treatment and there are many effective community-based programmes committed to reducing violence against women and children. Given the inefficiencies and uneven coverage of the region's judicial systems, many communities have even developed their own dispute resolution mechanisms, some of which involve restorative justice principles. Many of both the more established non-governmental organizations and the smaller, community-based groups are woefully underfunded and may well deserve more extensive international support to promote effective and long-term changes to the entrenched social problems of crime and drugs in Southern Africa.

Arising out of the experience of the United Nations Office on Drugs and Crime of the past three years in the region, the following crime- and drug-related priorities enjoy broad regional support as areas for enhanced training and technical assistance in partnership with the international donor community:

(a) Development of and assistance to national crime prevention, criminal justice and anti-corruption strategies, including enhanced collection of data and sharing of information on the crime and drug situation within and among each SADC member State so as to allow analysis and publication of crime statistics and substance abuse and other drug-related data, which in turn will inform realistic and achievable national and regional crime prevention and drug control strategies and anti-corruption strategies;

(b) Enhanced legislative and judicial capacities, including harmonization of both national legislation and SADC protocols with the United Nations conventions on drug control and crime prevention, in particular the Organized Crime Convention, and increased criminal justice system capacities and improved court management, including development of juvenile justice systems and diversion options, so as to prevent harsh, long-term social consequences, relieve prison overcrowding and promote social reintegration;

(c) Promotion of initiatives involving the prevention of both crime and drug abuse, including campaigns to raise public awareness of drug- and crime-related problems;

(d) Targeted support to operational law enforcement, including an audit of basic equipment and training requirements to combat cross-border crime and drug trafficking in order to deploy more effectively the limited resources available, leading to an enhanced capacity to interdict the flow of contraband and illicit drugs, disrupt market opportunities for organized criminals and apprehend criminal syndicate leaders, so as to reduce other forms of violent and serious crime, including violence against women and children; and development and extension of targeted training programmes for law enforcement and anti-corruption agencies;

(e) An audit of treatment and rehabilitation capacities in order to strengthen treatment facilities, reinforce prison management and broaden reintegration programmes, for which minimum standards and best practices should be developed for the population at large, as well as prison populations;

(f) Linking each of the five priorities above to sustainable development, especially in rural areas, in particular sustainable development of legitimate income-generating activities and the rule of law.

Conclusion

Obviously each country in Southern Africa has its own set of needs and priorities for international technical assistance. However, a regional analysis of those singular needs and priorities, as well as those identified by the regional organizations and informed by the views of the non-governmental organization community, should lead to a more focused and integrated programme of international technical assistance. It should allow for increased synergy, identification of existing gaps, and reduction of waste and duplication. In the experience of the Regional Office for Southern Africa of the United Nations Office on Drugs and Crime, while the needs of most regional players, whether governmental or non-governmental, whether enforcement-driven or prevention-driven and whether politically or developmentally focused, are great in the crime prevention and criminal justice arena, so too are their interests in forming genuine partnerships with the international technical assistance community. It is hoped that the analysis contained in the present article will provide the basis for encouraging positive action towards developing such partnerships, within and among each of the countries in the region.

References

1. Mark Shaw, "Regional trafficking: towards an understanding of West African criminal networks in Southern Africa", *African Security Review*, vol. 10, No. 4 (2001).
2. United Nations Office on Drugs and Crime, Regional Office for Southern Africa, *South Africa: Country Profile on Drugs and Crime* (Pretoria, 2002).
3. Charles Goredema, ed., *Organised Crime in Southern Africa: Assessing Legislation*, Institute for Security Studies, Monograph No. 56 (June 2001).
4. Ugljesa Zvekic, ed., *Corruption and Anti-Corruption in Southern Africa: Analysis Based on the Results of the Regional Seminar on Anti-Corruption Investigating Strategies with particular regard to Drug Control for SADC Member States* (Pretoria, United Nations Office on Drugs and Crime, Regional Office for Southern Africa, 2002).

5. Alice Hills, *Policing Africa: Internal Security and the Limits of Liberalization* (Boulder, Colorado, Lynne Rienner, 2000).
6. Dirk van Zyl Smit and Frieder Dünkel, eds., *Imprisonment Today and Tomorrow: International Perspectives on Prisoners' Rights and Prison Conditions* (New York, Aspen Publishers, 2001).
7. Wilfred Schärf, "Regional report: Africa", paper presented at the international conference entitled "Penal Reform: a New Approach for a New Century", Egham, United Kingdom of Great Britain and Northern Ireland, 13-17 April, 1999.